ILLEGITIMA

An Examination of Bastardy

ILLEGITIMACY

An Examination of Bastardy

Jenny Teichman

Cornell University Press
Ithaca, New York

For information address Cornell University Press, 124 Roberts Place, Ithaca, New York 14850.

First published 1982 by Cornell University Press

Published in Great Britain under the title
Illegitimacy: A Philosophical Examination

International Standard Book Number 0-8014-1491-1
Library of Congress Catalog Card Number 81-70703

Printed in Great Britain

Contents

Preface

I have found from experience that readers usually suppose that books about illegitimacy have to be either pleas for reform or cries of woe sent up to the public on behalf of unmarried mothers and their 'blossoms in the dust'. This book, however, is neither a plea for reform nor a cry of woe; it is, rather, a philosophical and factual description of an idea and a set of institutions. The idea, it seems to me, is much more complex than it is usually taken to be. It depends, furthermore, on complex institutions – what anthropologists call 'structures' – and it cannot be properly described unless these too are described. As far as I know, no philosopher to date has attempted an analysis of the idea of illegitimacy. I have here attempted a philosophical description of illegitimacy partly because it is a complicated idea, partly because it is a misunderstood idea and partly because it is an idea of considerable human importance.

Acknowledgements

I would like to thank Angela Hamblin for permission to reprint several passages from her monograph *The Other Side of Adoption* (London, 1977). I am also grateful to Gillon Aitken, Ltd for permission to quote from Frank Norman's *Banana Boy* (London, 1969).

CHAPTER 1

Definition, Meaning, Explanation

What is illegitimacy? There is more than one kind of answer to this question. One way of answering the question is to give a dictionary definition. Another way is to describe the purpose, point or function of the legitimate/illegitimate distinction. A third way is to give as complete an account as possible of the role of this distinction in human life.

THE MEANING OF THE WORD

The *Oxford English Dictionary* defines 'illegitimate' as:

1. not authorized by law; irregular, improper;
2. not born in lawful wedlock, bastard;
3. not correctly deduced or inferred.

And it defines 'bastard' as:

1. (child) born out of wedlock or of adultery, illegitimate;
2. (of things) authorized, hybrid, counterfeit.

The same dictionary says that bastard is derived from Old French *ba(s)t*, which means baggage generally and particularly a kind of pack-saddle which could be used as a rough bed by a muleteer or other traveller, plus the ending —ard, a suffix which commonly forms derogatory nouns, such as 'sluggard', 'drunkard'. *Ba(s)t* is also the root of 'batman', which originally meant 'luggage-man', i.e., a servant in charge of an army officer's luggage.

It is not altogether clear why an illegitimate child should be called a baggage-child. Maybe the baggage in question was the father's luggage and an emblem of his short stay in town, like a commercial traveller's suitcase. Or perhaps the bag or baggage is the child's mother – thus labelled as a disreputable woman. Or again, perhaps the baggage or pack-saddle is the place of conception, the temporary bed symbolizing a temporary sexual union. In German the word for bastard is *Bänkling*, meaning 'bench-child' – presumably, a child begotten on a bench instead of in a proper marital bed. *Bänkling* may be related to the archaic English 'bantling', which means 'brat'. 'Brat' itself is Welsh.

It can be seen from the above that the etymology of the word 'bastard' makes only sidelong reference to the illicit character of the parents' union.

The word 'bastard' is normally used as an insult, but nowadays, it seems, that is not because it is equivalent in meaning to 'illegitimate person'. On the contrary, anyone who wants to use 'bastard' in place of 'illegitimate person' will have to explain that he means it in the literal sense. The literal sense is, in a way, no longer the primary sense, nor is it necessarily insulting; it can be argued that when the descriptive term 'illegitimate' is thought of as insulting, it is because it is perceived as formally equivalent to the offensive word 'bastard', not the other way round. Its offensiveness, then, has nothing to do with any reference to illicit birth.

'Bastard' is more than an insult; it is also a bad word, vulgar, coarse, obscene, almost a swear word. 'Bastard' is bad language, whereas 'illegitimate' is not. Hence red-blooded he-men use the word 'bastard' continually, sometimes even as a term of endearment.

In the summer of 1976 *The Times* published several letters about artificial insemination and illegitimacy. One correspondent urged that the word 'bastard' be abolished from the English language. He wrote: 'Bastard is an ugly word and reflects on the user more than on his target.' A few days later Somerset Herald, who is probably interested mainly in the bastards of Kings, also wrote to *The Times*. He said: 'It is nonsense to say that "bastard" is an ugly word; but no doubt it depends on the social level from which one regards the matter.' However, the fact that genealogists think of the word as a useful tool of their trade is not in itself enough to remove its bad aura.

'Bastard' has a bad aura, almost like an obscenity or a curse, but 'illegitimate' is not completely neutral. It seems probable that 'illegitimate' first came into general use as a euphemism, and, like certain other euphemisms, it has gradually collected some of the overtones of the word it replaced. Indeed, among some progressive people 'bastard' is all right (provided it is not used in its literal sense) but 'illegitimate' is taboo, like 'nigger'. There is an example of this taboo in a book called *Norway's Families*, edited by T.D. Eliot and A.R. Hillman.[1] Eliot and Hillman say that they 'do not believe' that there is any such thing as illegitimacy. Since illegitimacy is, in part, a legal status, their claim is about as sensible as saying that one does not believe that there are such things as plaintiffs or legatees. Probably what Eliot and Hillman really mean is that they do not believe that the distinction between legitimacy and illegitimacy is a good thing to have. They go on to say that they will never use the word 'illegitimate' except when quoting other authors and then very reluctantly. They apologize for the exception. One chapter of their book is called 'Non-Wedlock Situations in Norway', and they make heroic efforts to use the circumlocution 'child born in a non-wedlock situation': but sometimes they weaken and write 'illegitimate' instead. (However, they always in such cases place the word in inverted commas.)

It is the official policy of the National Council for One-Parent Families (NCOPF) in England never to use the word 'illegitimate' in its publications.

An examination of the dictionary definition, the etymology and the general aura of a word may tell us a lot or a little about a concept. It really all depends on what the word is. The dictionary definition of a word such as 'doll', for instance, will probably tell us most of what there is to know about the concept, mainly because there is not a great deal to know anyway. The case is otherwise with words such as 'proposition', 'mind', 'necessity', 'law', 'legitimacy', etc. In such cases a purely linguistic enquiry can tell us something about the concepts but not a great deal. Thus, when a pair of words marks a difference – e.g., legal/illegal, or slave/freeman, or citizen/alien – a dictionary, however excellent, will not explain the point of the distinction; and if we do not understand the point of the distinction we do not perfectly grasp the concept.

THE SIGNIFICANCE OF ILLEGITIMACY

About 8 or 9 per cent of people in Britain are born out of wedlock. This proportion is in no way atypical or startling. Over Europe as a whole over the last 100 years the proportion has varied from between 2 and 3 per cent (in Eire most of the time), 13 per cent (in Bavaria just before the First World War), up to 37 per cent (in Sweden in 1979). Quite a few people born out of wedlock are legitimized before they grow up, either by the subsequent marriage of their parents or by adoption. Of those who remain illegitimate, many suffer from some degree of social, legal and financial disadvantage. Even in the quite recent past the stigma of illegitimacy was very heavy and the disabilities very great. Willie Hamilton, MP for Fife, when speaking in the House of Commons in 1978 on a Bill designed to 'abolish illegitimacy',[2] broke down and wept as he described the penury and ostracism suffered in childhood by his wife, who was born illegitimate. This kind of pain and sorrow is hidden from most of us most of the time, just as illegitimacy itself is hidden. It is true that legal disabilities have been reduced in many of the countries of Western Europe and that ostracism is quite out of date in progressive circles, but it would be parochial indeed to suppose that the stigma and disadvantages have everywhere been totally abolished. There is also the question of whether the stigma of illegitimacy can be totally abolished, and even, supposing it can, of whether it ought to be.

The fact that quite a large number of people are born out of wedlock and the fact that this usually entails some disadvantage (or even positive suffering) are enough to show that illegitimacy has importance – importance, that is to say, in the sense of being of human concern, like crime, or poverty, or transplant surgery. But its importance (in the sense of its *point*) is not revealed by these facts. The point of the legitimate/illegitimate distinction is not to cause suffering; rather, it has to do with certain widespread human aims connected with the regulation of sexual activities and of population.

Human beings control the reproduction of their farm animals and domestic pets for a variety of reasons and in a number of different ways. The main reasons are to increase numbers, to decrease numbers, to maintain numbers and to improve the quality of stock. The means of control include the physical separation of male and female animals, the killing of young male animals (farm stock) or of young female animals (unpedigreed pets), artificial insemination, sterilization and castration.

Human beings also control, and probably always have controlled, the reproductive activities of their own species. The means used are more various and include, of course, the influence of law, religion, custom and ideology generally. The physical means are not dissimilar to those used with animals, which is not surprising, since human beings are an animal species. These physical means include sexual abstinence (voluntary or enforced), the separation of males and females (e.g. in boarding schools, workhouses, convents, prisons), contraception, abortion and infanticide. The control that human beings exercise over the reproductive activity of their own species is not aimed only at control of numbers. It is rarely overtly aimed at 'improving the stock'. The main aims of control include the organization of people into families, kin-groups and tribes; the support of children; and the preservation of a real or imagined racial or religious group identity. Marriage itself is a kind of reproduction regulator; indeed, it could be called a form of birth control, since marriage law of any kind effectively prevents some people from reproducing while encouraging others. Thus in polygamous societies, for example, men who are of royal blood or who are very rich beget many children, while those who are slaves or are poor beget few or none. Laws which raise or lower the minimum age of marriage, which prevent or permit divorce, which forbid or enforce marriage between cousins, which outlaw marriage between blacks and whites, or between Catholics and Protestants, or between Islamic women and non-Islamic men – all such laws prevent some couplings and conceivings, discourage others and encourage yet others.

Population control, when this merely means attempts to

stabilize or increase or decrease numbers, is not, in my view, inherently good or bad; but the means may be either all right or bad, and the circumstances may make the aim itself good or bad. It would be wrong, surely, to try deliberately to increase the population of a country (e.g., by means of some law) if the country were already overpopulated, and wrong, also, to try to further reduce the population of a twenty-first century world emptied by nuclear war. In different imaginable circumstances the attempt to change population numbers one way or the other could be sensible and laudable. As to the means, some are all right and some are not. Some of those actually used, especially in the past, were often fairly nasty, as a matter of fact. It is well-known that the Greeks and Romans both practised infanticide; indeed, the exposure of an unwanted infant is the beginning of some extremely famous myths. Female infanticide is more common than male infanticide and more common than a general culling: thus the human race treats itself more as it treats unpedigreed pets than as it treats farm animals. Female infanticide was mentioned by the Prophet Mahomet, who condemned it.[3] It was practised by the Eskimo, by some Australian Aboriginal tribes and by the Chinese. (As a matter of fact, Chinese attitudes have not changed as much as Mao Tse-tung, allegedly a feminist, would have wished: according to *The Times*, in one of its science reports of 1977, Chinese married couples in some towns were being offered a test of the amniotic fluid before deciding about abortion. This test shows the sex of the foetus as well as the presence of certain genetically determined defects. Hospital statistics in China showed that when the parents knew of the sex of the foetus 87 per cent of the females were aborted but only a small minority of the males.)

St Augustine spoke of lust as 'cruel'. Was he thinking of rape and sadism, or the lust of men brutal by nature or brutalized by circumstances? It seems not: he was talking about the infanticide made necessary – or apparently made necessary – by the occurrence of unregulated sex.[4] It is true that he did not differentiate between infanticide and abortion, but it is plain that he was referring to both.

In the past, then, infanticide was a common method of birth control. As to the future no one can say, but novelists sometimes make a guess. In *Brave New World*[5] Aldous Huxley supposed that future generations would control population by pills and also by breeding sterile human beings. In a later book, *Ape and Essence*,[6] the same author describes a world in which the deformed survivors of a nuclear war have to submit all their infants to a board of examiners made up of experts. These experts, each one a witch-doctor, scientist and priest, decide which infants shall live and which shall die. The infants are assessed according to a schedule which lists the permitted number of genetic defects, so that a child with 12 fingers and six nipples is allowed to live; more fingers or nipples than that means death. Meanwhile the parents are ceremoniously beaten with bulls' pizzles just to remind them that reproduction is a serious matter. . . . Huxley's first futuristic novel came partly true, as far as population control was concerned, in his own lifetime; it would be unpleasant if his later prediction also turned out to be correct.

Our own civilization, i.e., the civilization founded on Jewish and Christian traditions, has never officially permitted infanticide but has controlled population by regulating sexual activity (sometimes fairly strictly) and (recently) by allowing contraception and abortion.

Whatever means are used to control population and however complex the aim, the existence of a system of regulation and control must of necessity generate the concept of 'a child which ought not to have been born'. Ideological means, such as marriage laws, generate the concept of 'people who ought not to mate (or not with each other)'. Normally these two ideas go together to some extent, though they don't have to. A racist's idea of 'a child which ought not to have been born' is a half-caste: whether a half-caste's parents happen to be married or not is not the racist's primary concern. A eugenicist's idea of 'a child which ought not to have been born' is a child with inherited physical or mental defects. In over-populated countries, society's idea of 'a child that ought not to have been born' may include the third, fourth or later children of properly married couples. The traditional idea in our own society, however, is economic, as it were, so that ' a child which ought not to have been born' is, in the consciousness of people in the West, a child which will have no one to care for it and protect it, an 'unwanted child', a child who will become a burden to the state and the taxpayer and, in all probability, a misery to itself; in other words, a child with no legal claim on a breadwinning (male) parent – an illegitimate child.

EXPLAINING ILLEGITIMACY

In explaining phenomena we commonly refer to efficient or immediate causes. Thus to explain an epidemic of physical disease, for example, we may refer to germs and bad housing and poor nutrition, these being items which, taken together, are capable of explaining certain kinds of outbreak of disease; they are causes or causal factors. Reference to germs and poor nutrition, etc., does not merely re-describe the phenomenon to be explained: such reference is not that kind of explanation. A disease is a natural phenomenon: social phenomena are less easy to explain causally, and their supposed causal explanations have an embarrassing tendency to turn into vacuous redescriptions. That is not to say that social phenomena have no immediate or efficient causes. Given the existence of legitimacy versus illegitimacy as a social distinction, it still makes sense to ask: why, for what (immediate) cause, does one person have an illegitimate child and another person not? There may be an answer of a causal-covering-law kind to this question. On the other hand, there may be as many immediate causes as there are individuals involved. In any case, the search for immediate causes is mainly the job of social workers and (possibly) sociologists.

In considering social phenomena quite another kind of explanation, which could also be called causal in a sense, is possible as well. Kingsley Davis has argued[7] that a proper understanding of a social phenomenon such as illegitimacy can only be achieved by examining the role which the idea or institution (i.e. in this case, the idea or institution of legitimacy versus illegitimacy) plays in human society. Davis is a sociologist, but it seems to me that the kind of enquiry which he advocates is best described as applied philosophy, and the kind of explanation he recommends could be called the description of formal causes.

Now, pure philosophy consists in the examination of notions which are either very general and not special to any one area of human life or thought, or else are special, for either methodological or traditional reasons, to philosophy itself. Thus pure philosophy examines notions like cause, time, space, number, on the one hand and, on the other hand, notions like proof, implication, Universals and immortality. But applied philosophy examines notions which are to some extent special to some particular named or unnamed area of human thought or human life. Of course, the idea of a particular area is, in this context, somewhat vague; nevertheless, it is obvious enough that aesthetics, jurisprudence and social philosophy are branches of applied philosophy, while logic and metaphysics are branches of pure philosophy. Some pieces of applied philosophy fall under no named branch of the subject. Thus some philosophers have examined the ideas of the unconscious, the ego, the id; others have investigated the notions of rational choice, supply and demand, and the unseen hand. The philosophy of psychoanalysis and the philosophy of economics do not, however, have any special names. The fact that a branch of philosophy is called the philosophy of such-and-such does not necessarily show, on the other hand, that it is a branch of applied philosophy. Philosophical logic is sometimes called philosophy of logic, and some questions in metaphysics are sometimes called questions in the philosophy of religion – but whatever the labels may suggest, the philosophy of the logic and the philosophy of religion are branches of pure philosophy and, indeed, connected with each other. Roughly speaking, philosophy in the English-speaking world tends to be pure philosophy, apart from its continued interest in the philosophy of science, while European philosophy (e.g. existentialism, Marxism, structuralism) tends to be applied philosophy.

A common (but not a universal) feature of applied philosophy is that it requires some understanding of human institutions. This is obviously the case with jurisprudence, for example. In a sense, all philosophy concerns itself with institutions in so far as all philosophy concerns itself with language. But language is an institution only in a very broad sense of the word; it is not a specialized institution as is, say, the law.

A proper analysis of the notion of illegitimacy – that is, of the distinction between legitimacy and illegitimacy – requires not only a description of ideas and language but also a description of the human institutions which generate the ideas and give rise to the relevant meanings. The institutions which give rise to the legitimate/illegitimate distinction, and which thus create the logic of those ideas, are both specialized and manifold. In other words, the logic of these ideas is created by several different human institutions which act together, as it were. And the notion or distinction itself can be regarded as an institution, one that rests on other institutions and has its own point or purpose within a system of human arrangements.

It will be agreed by all that illegitimacy is not a natural attribute; it is not like featherlessness or fecundity. Rather, it is a status, like kingship or slavery or bankruptcy. Many animal species live in herds, with herd leaders that boss the others around; some species establish a pecking order between individuals; others make what zoologists call 'territorial claims'. These are social facts about animals. But it is obvious that a really complicated social status, like that of being illegitimate, being a slave, being a king, can only arise in a human society.

The legitimate/illegitimate distinction is situated at a multidimensional interface of human institutions and natural facts about human beings. These institutions and natural facts are: sex – reproduction – birth control; kinship – lineage – identity and names; inheritance – property – law; legality – morality – religion. The interest of the distinction consists precisely in the fact that it is situated at this interface.

CHAPTER 2

Causes

OUTSIDERS AND DEVIANTS

Illegitimacy is widely regarded as a suitable subject for sociological research. The more modest kind of research on this topic concentrates on the effects, especially the economic effects, of illegitimate birth. Study of the effects of illegitimate birth is nowadays encouraged, publicized and, in many cases, sponsored and paid for by various public and private organizations – for example, by the NCOPF, by the Institute for Community Studies, by certain university departments and by the Medical Research Council (MRC). A more ambitious and more contentious kind of research, also sometimes sponsored by medical, educational and other bodies, studies not the effects but the possible causes of illegitimacy. Attempts to 'explain' illegitimacy are made by medical sociologists, deviance theorists and criminologists. By tradition 'criminology' is, in fact, the academic heading under which illegitimacy is most likely to become a subject of learned investigation.

When research looks at effects it is liable to concentrate on the child rather than on the mother; conversely, when it looks for causes it tends to concentrate on the mother rather than on the child.

The assumption behind explanatory sociological research seems to be that the normal is uncaused, or at any rate needs no explaining, whereas what is abnormal or unusual must have causes of some kind. Why people keep the rules needs no explanation or even can have no (interesting) explanation – so it is assumed – but the breaking of rules must have a cause or causes. Thus certain rule breakers or seeming rule breakers are lumped together as deviants or outsiders and become the objects of research.

Outsiders or deviants are created initially by social forms and social forces. It may be that some individuals actually choose the role of outsider because they like to feel different or want an opportunity to exercise the virtue of courage, but they can only make such a choice because there are social forms and forces to disagree with or repudiate in the first place. The role of outsider, which merges with that of the tolerated eccentric, can be quite enjoyable in a tolerant, civilized community, but in an intolerant society ostracism and persecution of outsiders can be very severe and hardly enjoyable for the victim. Positively choosing to oppose, or to remain in opposition to, the community at large needs courage in most places; hence those who do this often have strong moral or religious convictions which they intend to abide by, come what may. Other outsiders are outsiders because they have taken a risk or because they have been elected to the role by a community which has a need to persecute: in these cases, of course, no positive choice is involved.

Outsiders fulfil a useful and, arguably, a necessary role on the edges of societies. Ishmael went into the desert, and by doing that, he showed everyone else where the desert was and reminded them too how cosy and pleasant it is to stay at home and be an insider. The outsider strengthens the herd instinct of the insiders by being an object lesson; he reinforces the cohesion that holds the community together. Every group needs such reinforcing now and then; hence every group – every suburb, village, school, club, office, university faculty and so on – has to elect an outsider from time to time. Because outsiders hold groups together by being object lessons, it is ideologically necessary that outsiders should be, or at least should appear to be, unhappy, and this is part of the reason why outsiders have to be persecuted. Another part of the reason is that the persecution is itself a group activity in which individual insiders can demonstrate their loyalty to the group and its mores. This can be seen at all levels of social life: for example, by ostracizing illegitimate individuals and unmarried mothers, one demonstrates one's own legitimacy and one's loyalty to the sexual and property laws of the community; conversely, by stating that all references to illegitimacy are mere shibboleths, one demonstrates one's loyalty to the ideals of the permissive society.

RESEARCH

Early research: Percy Kammerer

Percy Kammerer's book entitled *The Unmarried Mother* was based on research carried out in America between 1915 and 1917 and published in 1918 as a *Criminal Science Monograph*.[1] In his preface he writes: 'There lie under my hand today cold abstracts of many lives which stress and passion have led to mistaken ends in which the reader may more readily perceive the element of tragedy than the note of hope.' Kammerer's book 'is based on a thorough analysis of five hundred cases secured from various sources' and describes 69 of the cases in some detail. The sources were, in fact, mainly the records of private charitable organizations, and Kammerer was astute enough to realize that his research would not have much application to women who were well-off enough not to need help from a private charity or the state.[2] (He has not been given any credit for this by later sociologists.) From the records 'each trait or factor working in the girl's environment in a given case, both for good and for bad, was noted on an individual slip of paper until some 60 or 70 slips had accumulated from each case.' Kammerer had to invent his own method of enquiry and appears to have coined the phrase 'case study'[3] to describe it. He also calls his procedure 'a literal use of the inductive method'.

He sorts the 'traits or factors' under 13 main headings, each of which has several sub-headings; the final result can only be described as a glorious schemozzle, which inadvertently paints a lurid picture of American domestic life but completely fails to generate any satisfactory causal or even probabilistic laws. The reason is that Kammerer discovers far too many 'traits and factors' existing in far too many combinations and permutations; furthermore, each named 'trait or factor' turns out to be such to cover, in fact, a huge range of 'traits or factors'. For example, 'Bad Home Conditions' includes, at one end of the scale, parents who sell their daughters' sexual favours for cash to lodgers, parents who run brothels and parents who commit incest and, at the other end of the scale, a guardian, a well-off and friendly aunt, who is 'too lenient'.[4] Again, 'heredity' covers anything from 'mother also had illegitimate child' and 'parents' marriage was forced' to 'comes from a family who have been paupers and criminals for over one hundred and fifty years'. (101 members of this family are listed, including great-uncles, cousins, great-great-grandfathers, all of whom were alcoholic, syphilitic, feeble-minded, immoral, tubercular, neurotic, paralytic, criminal, suffering from cancer or confirmed runaways, or several of these. The rest died in infancy.)[5] 'Demoralizing recreation' similarly covers a wide range of things, from 'the contaminating influence to be found in . . . the motion-picture theatres' to the presence of floating brothels, which, it seems, used to sail up and down Lake Michigan disguised as ordinary excursion steamships and ferries, and which (according to Kammerer) young girls quite often boarded in error, with serious consequences.[6]

Kammerer's 14 principal possible causal factors are:

1. Bad Home Conditions;
2. Bad Environment;
3. Bad Companions (there turn out in the main to be men who make promises of marriage and then run off, and married men who pretend to be single);
4. Early Sex Experience;
5. Mental Abnormality;
6. Sexual Suggestibility;
7. Heredity;
8. Recreational Disadvantages;
9. Educational Disadvantages;
10. Physical Abnormality;
11. Abnormal Sexualism;
12. Mental Conflict;
13. Sexual Suggestibility by One Individual (presumably, falling in love);
14. Assault, Rape, Incest.[7]

Kammerer does not arrange these causative factors (so-called) into any hierarchy or chain, though one might suppose that the third (bad companions) combined with the thirteenth (sexual suggestibility by one individual) ought to be given a special position in any causal account.

Although Kammerer's study does not in the end yield anything like an 'explanation' of illegitimacy, and although it is sometimes self-contradictory, it has to be admitted that his case-histories make extraordinarily interesting reading and are in their own way instructive. They throw a lurid but perhaps not altogether distorting light on American life in the early part of this century. Here is one of his 69 examples:

> *Case 24:* This (Norwegian) girl came to Boston alone at the age of 17. . . . There was some difficulty regarding her permission to land in this country, but when finally allowed to do so she sat on a nearby rock and began to cry. Some sailors from the ship found her and sent her to an immigrants' home, where she remained till all her money was spent. . . . for days she looked for work, often without food, spending the nights in doorways . . . . she met a Swedish policeman. . . . and he secured her a position in a hotel. . . . This girl is a pleasant clean and wholesome type, always laughing. . . . Her difficulty lay in not being able to be good and have a good time as well. . . . While working at the hotel the girl saw a good deal of a young man who was frequently away, and was looking forward to marrying him. . . . one evening a girlfriend invited her to spend the evening with some sailor friends of hers, and after some singing and general boisterousness she was further prevailed upon to spend the night with one of them. . . . when the girl objected he told here not to mind, that all women were sexually immoral. Since that time the man has asked her to marry him but she has refused. . . . after much discouragement the girl went away with a (third) man who worked on a nearby farm, with an evident desire to provide a father for her child. . . . unfortunately he proved to be already married. . . . he was arrested and is now serving a sentence for bigamy.[8]

Kammerer comments: 'Little is known about the girl's parents (in Norway) save that the mother has buried three husbands. Her influence over her daughter does not seem to have been a very good one. . . .' and gives as his diagnosis of this case the following improbable deduction:

> Causative factors: (a) Bad home conditions: Mother loose, gave girl no standards. Came to this country at 17. (b) Bad environment; alone at 17. Poverty. (c) Bad companions: Led into immorality by promiscuous girl. (d) Recreational disadvantages: No friends.[9]

Kammerer's diagnosis of other cases include the following:

> *Case 20:* Causative factors: (a) Bad home conditions: Father hunchback. Mother died when girl 16. Father away three evenings a week. Young men called when father away. (b) Bad companions: Young man called against father's wishes. (c) Recreational disadvantages: Girl worked too hard.[10]
>
> *Case 54:* Causative factors: (a) Mental conflict: Engagement broken because man found her to be illegitimate. Girl soon pregnant by another. (b) Bad home conditions: *Nothing known* of girl's parents. Girl boarded since 7 years old. (c) Heredity: *Mother and father immoral.* (My italics)[11]

Kingsley Davis

Kingsley Davis's work on illegitimacy[12] is far more analytic – even, more philosophical – than the work of other writers on the topic.

Davis says that research of the kind undertaken by, for example, Kammerer cannot explain illegitimacy. He argues that an explanation must make clear what the point of the legitimacy/illegitimacy distinction is, what role it plays in society. This is true, but giving an account of the role of a distinction does not make redundant other kinds of explanation. For instance, the distinction between the criminal and the non-criminal cannot be understood, of course, unless the notion of law is understood; the existence of law is a necessary condition of there being a distinction between the criminal and the non-criminal. All the same, to understand how the distinction comes about and what its point is is not to understand everything there is to understand about crime. The existence of law could be called the formal cause of crime, but it remains possible to investigate hypotheses about the immediate causes of criminal behaviour. On the other hand, it should not be forgotten that the hypothesis that criminal behaviour has no general causal explanation could turn out to be the best one.

Research in California: Clark E. Vincent

Vincent's book *Unmarried Mothers*[13] was published in 1963 and is based on Californian case studies. Vincent notes, first, the paucity of research on unmarried fathers, which he attributes partly to the 'double standard of morality' and partly to the fact that unmarried fathers are socially invisible, whereas unmarried pregnant girls are both socially and actually visible. (They are socially visible because they need obstetric and financial help.) Vincent's book includes a chapter on unmarried fathers which is devoted to proving that they are not 'sex exploiters'. He does not explain how or where he collected the samples for this chapter. Second, Vincent notes that although 33 of the American states have statutes which impose criminal sanctions on voluntary coition between unmarried adults, unmarried mothers in America are rarely, if ever, prosecuted; nor are unmarried fathers. This he attributes to humanitarianism. Third, Vincent points out that earlier research on illegitimacy and its causes always overlooked certain classes of unmarried mothers, usually those who had enough money to hide the birth of a baby by travelling to other states, or by attending private clinics, or both. He thinks that this was partly deliberate, a reflection of middle-class researchers' respectful attitudes to middle-class girls and their middle-class families. Finally, Vincent claims that researchers in the past have selected case histories which tend to confirm whatever hypothesis about illegitimacy happens to be fashionable at the time. Thus he claims that before 1930 researchers 'proved' that the causes of illegitimacy were immorality, bad companions and mental deficiency; in the 1930s it was 'proved' that the causes were broken homes, poverty and 'disorganized neighbourhoods'; in the 1940s and early 1950s it was 'proved' that the causes were psychological and psychiatric; and in the late 1950s, when researchers finally turned their middle-class attention to the middle classes, it was 'proved' that society itself was sick.

Vincent's own research findings are based on case histories

of girls and women from both working-class and middle-class backgrounds. However, he excludes from his study black women, women with more than one child, married and divorced women and rape victims. His findings (given those exceptions) tend to support the hypothesis that there are no significant social, economic or psychological differences between unmarried mothers and girls and married women in the same age groups. This does not mean that he rejects the idea of a causal explanation; it signifies only that he does not look for causes in the unmarried mother's immediate environment or in her psyche. His theory is that illegitimacy is, in a sense, a result of what he calls 'the philosophy of fun' or 'fun morality'.[14] This 'fun morality', he says, first appeared in the 1940s (so it is obvious that illegitimacy prior to that time will need some different kind of explanation). 'Fun morality' is reflected in the notion that a child will learn better if he is having fun, digest better if he likes the food and, in general, will lead a better life if life is full of fun. Young adults are taught that sex is fun, and since anything that is fun is automatically supposed to be good by people reared with fun, seeking out good sex encounters becomes part of the individual's personal ideology. 'Good sex is what it's all about', 'it' being the good life and life in general. Fun sex is sponsored by advertising and by business promotion (e.g., in the form of 'escorts' for visiting businessmen at conferences). Vincent says:

> The implementation of fun morality as a means to learning, child-rearing, and production goals. . . . serves as a source of permissive attitudes concerning illicit sexual relationships, making it possible for such attitudes to coexist unnoticed with censorious attitudes towards illicit pregnancies.[15]

He suggests that we should consider fun morality as demonstrating that illegitimacy can be an inadvertent by-product of a combination of means to conventional goals. Vincent shows no interest in explaining either illegitimacy outside America or any occurrences of the phenomenon prior to about 1940 (unlike Davis and Kammerer); nevertheless the above generalization would probably apply to communities existing outside Vincent's very narrow limits of space and time.

Research in Scotland: the MRC unit at Aberdeen

Research in Aberdeen into illegitimacy is carried out by the MRC's Medical Sociology Unit at the University of Aberdeen. By and large, it is based not on sampling but on studies of the records of all unmarried mothers in a population over a given period of time. The technique of basing research on all cases of a phenomenon found in a given area over a given period of time is used in the study of epidemic physical disease: thus it is not surprising that a research unit funded by the MRC should try to apply it to social phenomena.

One important and typical piece of research is Barbara Thompson's 1956 study[16] of the socio-economic status of all unmarried mothers who had children in Aberdeen in the years 1949–52, which indicated that illegitimacy and prenuptial conception occurred predominantly among the lower classes. Derek Gill claims[17] that Thompson's findings refute Vincent's supposition that unmarried mothers are not significantly different, psychologically or socially, from girls and young women in the same age group in the population at large. However, few would feel as happy as Gill does about making extrapolations from Aberdeen in 1952 to California in 1963, and it is only if such extrapolations are made that one piece of work can be deemed to refute the other. The technique of studying all cases of a phenomenon instead of merely samples leads inevitably to the study of samples of communities in place of samples of cases. It is not possible to study all cases in all communities because the number of illegitimate people in the world runs into scores of millions.

DISEASE, CRIME AND ILLEGITIMACY

Theoretically, the research techniques appropriate for studying epidemic disease could be used to study any reasonably prevalent human phenomenon at all, provided the phenomenon was properly recorded by statisticians. But the usefulness of the results cannot be taken for granted.

Epidemiological research into physical diseases can be used in the following ways:

1. to study the history of the health of human communities and the history of the rise and fall of diseases and any change in their seriousness, and to suggest extrapolations into the future which can then be tested as opportunities arise;
2. to diagnose the overall health of a community and the overall physical condition of its members by measuring the amount of ill-health, its distribution, incidence, prevalence, mortality, etc.;
3. to make an estimate of the likelihood of an individual's contracting this or that disease;
4. to complete the clinical picture of a chronic disease and to describe its natural history by following the course of remission, relapse, adjustment, disability and immunity;
5. to form hypotheses about the causes of disease and to test them as opportunity arises by studying the incidence of diseases in different groups at different times and so on;
6. to study the workings of the health services in a particular country;
7. to study the effects of disease on the economic and social situation of individuals.

The difference between disease and illicit pregnancy and birth can be seen from the fact that, for the latter, studies of the kind described above under points 1, 2, 3, 4 and 5 above are quite inappropriate.

1. When the existence and character of a phenomenon depend on laws and customs, extrapolations either into the future or to communities with different mores or habits cannot be made.
2. There is, in the case of pregnancy, no real parallel with 'the overall physical health of the community'.
3. Estimates of the probability of an individual's becoming illicitly pregnant are unlike estimates of the probability of an individual's contracting, say, measles or tuberculosis because the first is governed by choice as well as by chance: furthermore, the ratio of choice to chance varies in an incalculable way between individuals and even perhaps between communities.
4. The concepts of remission, relapse, adjustment and im-

munity do not apply to illicit birth (except possibly in some poetic or metaphorical way).

5. Hypotheses about causes are vitiated for the same reason that extrapolations for the future or for different places are vitiated.

However, this is not to say that 'epidemiological' research – i.e., social research using some of the methods appropriate to the study of epidemic disease – is of no use at all in sociological studies of illegitimacy. On the contrary, it is doubtless quite useful if its aim is to discover the economic and social effects (rather than the causes) of illicit birth (point 7) or the workings and effectiveness of the maternity services, the Department of Health and Social Security, private charities and statutes designed to alleviate the poverty and disadvantage which are generally associated with illegitimate birth (point 6). But good sampling techniques could also discover these things. Two examples of factual research into effects are Margaret Wynn's *Fatherless Families*[18] and Dennis Marsden's *Mothers Alone*;[19] these are not medically oriented or 'epidemiological', but they reveal a great deal about the phenomenon of illegitimate birth in Britain.

The statute which made fornication a punishable offence in England was repealed in 1834, as will be noted in a later chapter. In other countries, however, various kinds of fornication, particularly adultery, remained crimes until more recently. For example, in Austria until the First World War married women could be sent to prison for adultery, although their paramours were seemingly immune from punishment, so that sometimes a woman would be judged guilty and imprisoned on the word of an ungrateful lover or one determined on blackmail. In Spain under Franco a married woman who was unfaithful could be sent to prison, as could her lover, though a married man could be unfaithful (e.g., with a prostitute) without necessarily committing a crime. This law of Franco's times was repealed fairly soon after his death. In Europe (including Russia), North America and Australasia early statutes against adultery have either been repealed or are now treated as thoroughly dead letters. The study of illegitimacy by criminologists in these countries is therefore a somewhat anachronistic activity, to say the least.

Then has illegitimacy no causes, only effects? It does have causes – its formal causes are the institutions which generate the legitimate/illegitimate distinction, and its immediate causes are almost as multifarious as human motives and loves and hates. All research which tries to explain illegitimacy proves in the end that its immediate causes are multitudinous. That is not something that could have been taken for granted before the research was carried out; furthermore, to show that a phenomenon cannot be explained by reference to a causal or covering law may be just as useful and as significant as to show that it can.

CHAPTER 3

Illegitimacy and the Law

In the *Oxford English Dictionary*, as we have noted, a 'bastard' is defined as 'a child born out of wedlock' and 'wedlock' is defined as 'the married state'. Legitimacy and illegitimacy, therefore, are related to marriage. We run into a difficulty here because some anthropologists claim that it is impossible to give a universal definition of marriage.[1] What they mean is that the status (or statuses) recognized as marriage varies considerably from one country or community to another, being regulated in different places and at different times by different rules and prohibitions and carrying different duties, rights and obligations. However, we should take care to avoid the disadvantages of having too narrow a concept of definition. A universal definition, a single, simple set of necessary and sufficient conditions, is perhaps impossible, but a definition or description which consists of a list of criteria (including functional criteria), most or some of which must be present before an institution qualifies as marriage, obviously is possible. A definition of this kind will generate a distinction between central, or typical, or core cases on the one hand and borderline cases on the other; but this is not a defect of the definition, merely a consequence of the character of the concept defined. The fact that a 'strict' definition – for example, a definition in Euclidean geometry – does not generate a distinction between typical cases and borderline cases is not a defect either, but merely a consequence of the character of Euclidean concepts. I intend, therefore, to proceed on the assumption that marriage, legitimacy, illegitimacy, etc. can all of them be satisfactorily defined or described.

MARRIAGE

Marriage was the concern of religion long before it became the concern of the state. The presence of religious figures, such as priests, witch doctors, holy men or astrologers, and the invocation of supernatural beings, for example, gods or goddesses or the spirits of ancestors, are fairly common features of marriage ceremonies, as are ritualized feasting and dancing, special clothing and homilies by religious or other authorities. According to the Roman Catholic Church and others, marriage is a sacrament, 'a visible sign of spiritual grace', like baptism or confirmation.

Nevertheless, all modern states reserve the right to define which unions are legal marriages and which are not. Furthermore, whatever form the marriage institution takes, it always involves changes in the legal and social status of the marriage partners and in the kinship relations of their respective family groups. Marriage creates rights and duties of a legal or quasi-legal nature, and it also creates affinities, i.e. kinship based not on blood but extant 'in law'. Legitimacy and illegitimacy, therefore, being related to marriage, are also associated with the legal system. Here we come across more difficulties. There is no such thing as *the* legal system, since the world contains many legal systems, and most legal systems are anyway not static. Law making in the modern world is a continuous process, and modern legal systems are almost like living organisms; they change gradually all the time. Hence the best that can be done in describing the legal meaning of legitimacy and illegitimacy is to describe the place of these notions inside one system of law, while marking from time to time such divergences between that system and others which seem interesting. In what follows most (though not all) of the references are to English family law. English law is not only a developed system; it is also fairly widespread and fairly typical. It is widespread in that it is the historical progenitor of the legal systems of North America, Australasia, much of the Carribean area and some parts of Africa. It is typical in that it resembles in various ways the legal systems of the other countries of Europe, in contradistinction to Muslim, Soviet and traditional African systems.

According to Bromley,[2] 'the history of the English Law

relating to the formalities of marriage – and even the state of the Law immediately before the passing of Lord Hardwicke's Act in 1753 – is still a matter of considerable doubt.' Before the Council of Trent (*circa* 1563), however, it appears that no religious ceremony was needed to make a marriage: marriages could be made simply by the parties declaring to each other 'I . . . take you . . . as my wife/husband.' There was no lower age limit for marriage under canon law or common law, but marriages between children – i.e., girls under 12 and boys under 14 – became void when the parties reached those ages unless cohabitation began or was continued at that point. An Act of Parliament of 1929 fixed the lower age limit for marriage in England at 16 years.[3]

For a long time it had been the custom to contract marriages in the presence of a priest. This was usually done near the door of the church, and after the marriage the husband and wife would go into the church for nuptial mass. Common law favoured this sort of public marriage because the publicity made it easier to ascertain the existence of the union. The common law rights – e.g., as to inheritance – of the offspring depended on the existence of a proper union. Between the Council of Trent in the sixteenth century and Lord Hardwicke's Act in the eighteenth century there were three different methods by which a marriage could be contracted. The first, church marriage, was celebrated after the publishing of banns in the presence of a priest and in the presence of other witnesses. A person under the age of 21 was supposed to obtain parental consent for this type of marriage. The second, clandestine marriage, consisted in declaration in the presence of a priest, with no other witnesses, and was valid for persons under 21 even if celebrated without parental consent. The third, declaration followed by consummation, remained a valid method until 1753. Either party to a non-public marriage was entitled to obtain, if he or she wished it, an order from an ecclesiastical court to make the other party solemnize the marriage publicly.

Lord Hardwicke's Act laid down, first, that banns had to be published two weeks before the ceremony was to take place; second, that the marriage had to be solemnized in a parish church in the presence of a priest and two other witnesses; and third, that parental consent was necessary for persons under 21. Quakers and Jews were exempt from Hardwicke's second condition but Catholics and Dissenters were not. In 1836, however, alterations in the law allowed Catholics and Dissenters to marry in churches other than those of the Church of England.[4] At the same time registrars of marriages were created and registered buildings other than churches were designated as places in which marriages could be celebrated. Hardwicke's Act made Gretna Green a popular place for weddings for runaway couples, for the reason that Scotland continued to endorse the validity of marriages made by declaration in the presence of a witness, and England continued to recognize the validity of Scottish marriages. The size of this loophole was reduced somewhat in 1823, when an Act of Parliament made Gretna Green marriages and other marriages in Scotland void for English couples if both parties were knowingly trying to evade the provisions of English law.[5]

Under English law a formal defect does not automatically render a marriage void. But a marriage, whether formally correct or formally defective, can turn out to be either void or voidable for other reasons.

A void marriage is not the same thing as a voidable marriage. A void marriage is one which, strictly speaking, has never been a marriage at all. The offspring of a void marriage are illegitimate, and the survivor of such a union is not a widow or widower. The impediments which render a marriage void in England – and, indeed, in the other countries of Europe – relate respectively to age, to polygamy and to the prohibited degrees of blood relationship. Thus a marriage is void in English law if one party or both parties are under 16. Marriages between domiciled English persons and foreign persons that are celebrated outside England are usually void, though not invariably, if either party is under 16. Polygamous marriages are always void in England and are punishable as bigamy. However, the children of valid foreign polygamous marriages of non-English people who have settled in England count as legitimate. Such children, though, cannot inherit entailed estates, and social welfare payments in England are only paid for the children of potentially polygamous marriages – such as Muslim marriages – when the marriage is and always has been monogamous. Spokesman for certain migrant groups sometimes argue for changes to be made in English family law so that Muslims could contract valid polygamous marriages in England. Changes in tax law and social security regulations are also needed, it is claimed, if Britain's laws are to reflect the requirements of a truly multi-racial society. The third type of impediment which renders a marriage void is concerned with the prohibited degrees of relationship. These are set out in the Old Testament in Leviticus 18. There are now some minor differences between Roman Catholic and Anglican rules. The Anglican impediments were formalized by Archbishop Parker in 1563 and can be read in the *Book of Common Prayer*. It is well-known that peoples whose laws and customs are not based on Jewish–Christian tradition have rules and stipulations as to who may marry whom which differ greatly from European rules. Thus some Australian Aboriginal tribes forbid marriages between individuals who are so remotely related in blood, by our standards, as hardly to count as relatives at all; others discourage marriages except between cousins. The custom of the levirate found in polygamous communities in Africa and elsewhere puts a man under an obligation to marry his deceased brother's wife, a procedure forbidden in Leviticus:

> Thou shalt not uncover the nakedness of thy brother's wife: it is thy brother's nakedness.[6]

though not in Deuteronomy:

> If brethren dwell together, and one of them die, and have no child, the wife of the dead shall not marry without unto a stranger: her husband's brother shall go in unto her, and take her to him to wife, and perform the duty of an husband's brother unto her.[7]

The prohibitions relating to age, to polygamy and to the degrees of relationship obviously affect the question of who is and who is not legitimate. They also apply directly to illegitimate people who wish to marry. For example, an adopted person may not marry his adoptive parent even if the parent is not a blood relation. In other words, marriage with a parent is forbidden whether or not he or she is a 'real' parent. An adopted person is allowed to marry his adoptive sibling unless the sibling is related in blood as well as in law in a prohibited degree.

A voidable marriage is one that has been set aside by a decree of nullity from a competent court. The decree has retrospective effect, and for some (though not all) purposes the couple are then deemed never to have been married. Thus a decree of nullity differs from a divorce decree. Decrees of nullity were originally issued by ecclesiastical courts: in England the ecclesiastical courts lost this power in 1857.[8] While a void marriage has never been a marriage, a voidable marriage is a valid marriage until it is successfully challenged. If it never is challenged, then the offspring are legitimate and the survivor of the union is a widow or widower. The marriage remains in force until a decree is issued, and the parties are not free to marry others while it is in force. The parties to a void marriage, on the other hand, are really single and have the rights of single people. A marriage thought to be void can be challenged by anyone, including third parties, but a marriage thought to be voidable can only be challenged by one (or both) of the parties. Under common law the children of a marriage which had been declared null were rendered illegitimate retrospectively, but statutes of 1937,[9] 1949,[10] and 1965[11] have altered this, and now such children are deemed legitimate, other things being equal. As to marriages which have been declared void, it is now the case that the children of such marriages can apply for legitimate status. To succeed, the applicant must prove that at least one of his parents believed that the marriage was valid.

LEGITIMACY

Roman law, the law of Christendom (canon law) and English common law all adhere rigidly to the rule that the only children born legitimate are those who are born in wedlock, those who are conceived in wedlock and those who are both conceived and born in wedlock. Recent modifications in those parts of family law which govern the legitimation of children born illegitimate have not as yet affected this basic principle.

Common law and statute law in England both follow the maxim *pater est quem nuptiae demonstrant*; which is to say, the father of a child of a married woman is presumed to be her husband unless the contrary can be proved. The only exception to this rule is the child who is conceived during one marriage and born during another: he is presumed to be the (legitimate) child of the first husband. In some other countries – in West Germany, for instance – such a child counts as the legitimate offspring of the second husband.

The assumption that a married woman's child is the child of her husband can be rebutted, and, generally speaking, a rebuttal requires proof of no intercourse. In the past, when the legal and social disabilities of illegitimacy were very heavy, the proof had to be *beyond all reasonable doubt*, but nowadays the proof need be only *on the balance of probabilities.*[12] In England it is accepted that there is proof of no intercourse when a widow gives birth to a child more than ten months after the death of her husband; in some countries this period is allowed to be longer than ten months. Until 1969 mere separation was not regarded as proof of no intercourse, in that the absence of the husband at the presumed time of conception did not count against the legitimacy of the child unless the husband was outside the British Isles (the wife being at home, of course). A legal separation creates the presumption of no intercourse, but the presumption is rebuttable. In some countries the courts are able to order the parties involved in cases of disputed paternity to submit to blood tests. Blood tests can prove that a child is not someone's offspring but not that it is someone's offspring; hence such tests can prove illegitimacy but not legitimacy. A child cannot gain from such a test but may lose certain rights if the result proves illegitimacy or is indecisive. In England blood tests remain non-compulsory.

If a woman marries in late pregnancy the presumption is that the husband knows of the child and accepts it as his own, so the child will be deemed legitimate. However, if a woman marries in early pregnancy, and if her husband later rejects the child, the child will be judged illegitimate if the husband can give proper proof of no intercourse. The Poulett peerage case is cited as illustrating the legal principles involved. In 1849, on 23 June, Mr Poulett (later the sixth Earl Poulett) married Miss Elizabeth Newman. In August of that same year he left her and never lived with her again. On 15 December 1849 a son was born to Mrs Poulett, William T. T. Poulett. In 1846 Mr Poulett succeeded to the title. In 1871 his wife died, after which he married another lady. This second wife did not live long. In 1879 Lord Poulett married for the third time, and in 1883 his wife had a son, William J. L. Poulett. In 1899 Lord Poulett died and claims to the Poulett peerage were made by Mr William T. T. Poulett on behalf of himself, and by Rosa, Countess Poulett, on behalf of her young son, William J. L. Poulett, it being alleged that William T. T. Poulett was not the son of the sixth earl. A certain Dr Perks gave evidence that he had been present at the birth of Mr William T. T. Poulett. He stated that the boy had been a full-term child and not a premature infant. But perhaps the sixth earl begat the child before marrying its mother? If so the child, born as it was in wedlock, would have been legitimate. A Mrs Alexander, a friend of the first wife, then gave evidence. She said that the first Mrs Poulett had told her that Poulett was not the father of her son, the real father being a certain Captain Granville. A sworn statement made by Lord Poulett shortly before his death was then produced in court. In this statement the earl alleged that his first wife confessed to him soon after their marriage that she was pregnant by Captain Granville. Poulett also said in this document that he himself had had no sexual connection with the first Mrs Poulett prior to their marriage. The House of Lords then asked itself whether this testimony from the dead earl ought to be taken as evidence. For after all there was no possibility of cross-examining the earl; nor was the lady in the case in any position to reply, being also dead. However, in the end their lordships admitted the evidence: furthermore, they decided that the events of August 1849, the testimony of Perks and Alexander and the sixth earl's own deposition together constituted proof of no intercourse. In July 1903 the son of the third wife was declared to be the rightful heir.[13] It seems to me that the finding of the House of Lords was right *on the balance of probabilities* but perhaps not correct *beyond all reasonable doubt*.

It can be seen from this case that proof of no intercourse is a rather tricky matter. Another example which illustrates the point, though in a somewhat different way, is the dispute over the barony of Ampthill which was settled in 1976. The imbroglio began in 1921, when the first wife of the third Lord Ampthill gave birth to a son, Geoffrey. Lord Ampthill then attempted to divorce his wife for adultery, because, he said, he had never had sexual connection with her at any time. His wife defended the suit and produced medical testimony to the effect that she had been virgin until the time her son was born. Thus she too produced proof of no intercourse – that is to say, proof that she had never had intercourse with anyone, adulterous or otherwise. In English law it is not clear whether insemination by a non-husband and by means not involving intercourse is, strictly speaking, adultery. (Such insemination does not count as adultery in Scotland.) In any case, Lord Ampthill was not able to name any man as his wife's supposed lover: her case rested on the presumption that he himself was the genitor of the child. The divorce suit failed, and in 1926 the son was declared legitimate under the Legitimacy Declaration Act of 1858.[14] In 1976 the decree of legitimacy was upheld in the face of a challenge from the son of Lord Ampthill by a subsequent marriage.[15]

The desirability of some kind of procedure which would enable a disputed question of legitimacy to be settled once and for all led to the passing of the Legitimacy Declaration Act of 1858, alluded to above. This Act has been repealed but its provisions are incorporated in the Matrimonial Causes Act of 1965.[16] Under this law any person may petition for a decree that he is legitimate, or for a decree that his parents were properly married, or for a similar declaration that his grandparents were properly married. He must be a British subject or one whose right to be deemed a British subject depends on his legitimacy. It is not possible to petition on behalf of another adult person, nor can one petition to have another individual or oneself declared illegitimate under this law. Other countries have somewhat different rules (in West Germany, for example, it is possible to have oneself declared illegitimate).

There has been no ruling so far as to the status of a child conceived before its parents' wedding and born after the death of its father. According to the definition of a legitimate child as one either born in wedlock, or conceived in wedlock, or both, it would appear that such a child would be illegitimate. However, the current tendency of law making in the field of family law makes it very likely, I think, that if the case ever arises, some way will be devised of counting the child as legitimate.

ILLEGITIMACY

A woman who has never been married cannot, in any circumstances, give birth to a legitimate child. But a child conceived and born out of wedlock can be legitimated after its birth in one of several possible ways. These will be discussed in the next section.

A man who has never been married can, of course, beget a child who at its birth is deemed legitimate under the maxim *pater est quem nuptiae demonstrant*.

A widow can give birth to an illegitimate child, as already noted. In certain circumstances such a child can be legitimated after its birth.

A married woman with a living husband can give birth to an illegitimate child. Generally, but not always, such a child will be an adulterine bastard. For a child to count as illegitimate, it is normally necessary, though not of course sufficient, for its mother's husband to repudiate it. If the husband dies, those with an interest in his estate may in certain circumstances ask for a ruling by a competent court as to the legitimacy or otherwise of the wife's children.

Although the children conceived as the result of artificial insemination by donor (AID) are technically illegitimate, they are usually registered as the children of their mother's husband. Often the husband has agreed to AID and so, in a sense, has connived at hiding illegitimacy. For these reasons some people have argued that children conceived by AID might as well be regarded as legitimate in law. However, this leaves a problem about AID children conceived without the knowledge or permission of the mother's husband. Should they too be regarded as legitimate? This would place obligations of a legal nature upon the mother's husband which he might well consider unjust. In Scotland, in the case of McClellan, it was ruled that a wife who undergoes AID without her husband's consent commits no adultery. Nevertheless, the child is illegitimate, though not an adulterine bastard. Although a woman who undergoes AID in this kind of circumstance does not commit adultery with the donor, her action is wrong, it was ruled. No doubt AID could prove grounds for divorce if it were adjudged to be 'unreasonable behaviour'.[17]

A raped woman commits no adultery. Thus here too the child of a married woman which is not the child of her husband is illegitimate, but not an adulterine bastard. The principle involved is an ancient one; it is stated in Deuteronomy, where it is laid down that adultery shall be punished with death:

> But if a man find a betrothed damsel in the field, and the man force her, and lie with her: then the man only that lay with her shall die:
>
> But unto the damsel thou shalt do nothing; there is in the damsel no sin worthy of death. . . .[18]

Outside the Jewish–Christian tradition things can be quite different: in ancient Japan, for instance, a raped woman was regarded an either immoral or polluted – it is not clear which, nor whether the distinction made sense in Japan – and was expected to commit suicide.

Finally, the children of void marriages are illegitimate, as has already been noted. The children of voidable marriages found to be null were illegitimate under common law but, generally speaking (i.e., other things being equal), are deemed legitimate under modern English family law.

LEGITIMATION

Legitimation is not the same thing as a declaration or decree of legitimacy. A declaration of legitimacy – for example, one made under the 1858 Act already alluded to – decrees that the person concerned is, and always has been, the legitimate child of such-and-such parents. Once such a declaration has been properly and correctly issued it cannot be overturned. Legitimation, on the other hand, is a process in which the status of a child is altered, so that the child becomes legitimate after having been born illegitimate. In England a child who has been legitimated cannot be made illegitimate again. However, the possibility of repeated adoptions means that an individual might be the legitimate child of more than one set of parents at different times in its life.

The ways in which a child born illegitimate can be legitimated are as follows:

1. by an Act of King and Parliament designed specifically to legitimate a particular person or persons;
2. by the subsequent marriage of parents;
3. by adoption;
4. by suing for legitimacy under the acts of 1949 and 1965 (as described above, p. 28).[19]

Act of King and Parliament

It has always been possible under common law for the legislature to legitimate a particular illegitimate child, and there is no statute which removes this power. The power has not been exercised in modern times. Other countries also allowed for the legitimation of individuals in this way. Louis XIV of France, for example, legitimated several of his own bastards, and in the eighteenth century the king of Poland legitimated all the children in two Polish orphanages (it seems probable that the fathers of these children were known to be noble or royal). In England Richard II legitimated the illegitimate children of John of Gaunt. It could be argued, perhaps, that Elizabeth I legitimated herself. That Elizabeth was illegitimate to start with seems undeniable, since she was illegitimate according both to canon law and to the King and Parliament of England. In Henry VIII's First Succession Act of 1534[20] it was decreed that any children of Ann Boleyn were the king's 'lawful children' and 'right heirs'. However, in his Second Succession Act of 1536[21] it is stated that the marriage with 'the late Queen Anne' 'shall be taken, reputed, deemed and adjudged to be of no force, strength, virtue, nor effect', and that the issue of the marriage should be deemed illegitimate. At this point Elizabeth, already illegitimate by canon law, became illegitimate by Act of Parliament also, if that were possible. In his Third Succession Act of 1543,[22] however, Henry changed his mind again and decreed that in the event of the death of Prince Edward, the heirs to the throne were to be, in the first place, 'the Lady Mary, the King's Highness's daughter' and her lawful issue and, 'by default of such issue . . . the Lady Elizabeth the King's second daughter'. Henry's Third Act of Succession did not state overtly that the illegitimate Elizabeth had been made legitimate. Thus it can be argued that she was still illegitimate when she came to the throne. However, in 1559, the first year of her reign, the Act of Recognition of the Queen's Highness' Title to the Imperial Crown of this Realm[23] stated that Elizabeth was 'rightly, lineally and lawfully descended and come of the blood royal of this realm of England'. It could be argued that in signing and sealing this Act, Elizabeth legitimized herself.

Subsequent marriage of parents

Under Roman law a bastard was legitimized by the subsequent marriage of his parents provided that the parents had been free to marry each other at the time of his conception. Legitimation by subsequent marriage was also the rule under canon law. Alexander III, who was Pope from 1159 until 1181, claimed in connection with this matter: '*tanta vis est matrimonii ut qui antea sunt geneti post contractum matrimonium legitimi habitur*', which is to say, in effect, that marriage is such a powerful thing that it can work retrospectively and can legitimize the illegitimate. All the countries of Europe allowed legitimation by subsequent marriage, following canon law, with the notorious exception of England, which did not allow for this form of legitimation in its law until 1926. In 1235 an attempt was made to introduce a statute which would have brought England into line with the rest of Christendom on this matter, but it was defeated by the opposition of the temporal peers, who possibly decided that the property rights of heirs were best protected by very simple, rigid rules about legitimacy. However, in England during those centuries the bastard son of a couple who had married each other after his birth had a special place in the law. If such a son was the oldest known son of his father, and if he had grown up in the household of his (now married) parents, then he was able to take over the estate when his father died even if there happened to be another younger and legitimate son. An heir of this sort was known in the law as a special bastard, or *bastard eigne*.[24]

The Legitimacy Act of 1926,[25] alluded to above, provided that a child was legitimated by the subsequent marriage of its parents if both parents were free to marry at the time of its birth (not conception: cf. Roman law on this), subject to certain conditions about domicile. An Act of 1959[26] amended the above, so that now an illegitimate child can be legitimated by the subsequent marriage of its parents even if either or both were married to other persons at the time of its birth. Both Acts expressly state that a legitimated person shall have the same rights in respect of maintenance, inheritance and citizenship of the United Kingdom as a person born legitimate. However, in order to inherit an entailed estate a man must be legitimate under the old common law test.

Adoption

Under the Adoption of Infants Act of 1926[27] it became possible, for the first time, for parents to give up their parental rights in a clear and unambiguous way. Disparate laws on change of name, wardship, wills, even if invoked simultaneously, could not produce *adoption*.[28] The 1926 Act laid down rules whereby it became possible for the legal bond between a child and its natural parent(s) to be broken off and a new legal bond, that between the child and its adopter(s), established. In practice, the severance of the original legal bond affects more mothers than fathers, since the majority of children offered for adoption are illegitimate, and illegitimate children do not have a legal bond with their male parent anyway. In 1968 24,831 children were legally adopted in England, and of these 19,348 were illegitimate.

The 1926 Act was extensively criticized and extensively amended. Present law on adoption stems from the 1958 Adoption Act and includes the following main provisions.[29]

1. Only persons who are under the age of 18 and who have never been married can be legally adopted. Other countries have different rules; for example, it is possible in some places legally to adopt an adult in order to make him one's heir.

2. Persons adopting a child in England must be domiciled in England or Scotland. This, presumably, is designed to prevent the kind of international baby-snatching that some Far Eastern governments complained of immediately after the Vietnam–American war.
3. Adopters must be over 25 years of age unless they are already related to the child. The natural parents of an illegitimate child may adopt it at any age; other relatives of a child may adopt it if they are over 21.
4. Joint applications to adopt can only be made by persons who are married to each other.
5. A single man may not adopt a female child. Even the natural father can be refused permission to adopt a daughter. Thus in 1941 a man living alone was refused permission to adopt his natural daughter.[30]

A child cannot be adopted without the consent of its parent or guardian unless a court dispenses with this consent for special reasons. In this context 'parent' includes 'adoptive parent', since it is possible for a child to be adopted more than once. On the other hand, the presumption is that 'parent' does not include the natural father of an illegitimate child, although this matter has been under review for some years. Parental consent to adoption is not required if a competent court rules that the parent has failed to perform his or her parental duties – for example, when the parent has disappeared, or has abandoned the child, or has criminally ill-treated it through neglect or cruelty. It is also possible for the court to rule that consent is not needed in cases in which it is judged that consent has been withheld unreasonably. The following are examples. A man serving a life sentence for the murder of his wife refused to consent to the adoption of his legitimate child and was overruled on the grounds that in the circumstances it was unreasonable of him to withhold his consent.[31] In 1971 an unmarried West Indian woman domiciled in England refused to consent to the adoption of her third child. Lord Hailsham overruled her refusal on the grounds that the mother had no means of support other than the wages of her own female relatives 'and no male breadwinner'.[32]

Adoption is a process whereby statutory parents who, it is

supposed, will provide care and affection, are substituted for natural parents who for some reason are unable or unwilling properly to perform their parental duties. In England adoption is meant to give the adopted child the same rights, in regard to maintenance and inheritance, as those held by the legitimate, natural child of the adopters. It establishes legal rights and duties for the child and the adoptive parents, and in general has the effect of breaking off all existing legal ties between the child and its natural parents. Thus the adopters have a duty in law to maintain the child and cannot sue its natural mother or father for maintenance. The only exception is the case in which the natural mother herself adopts the child; she is allowed in law to sue the father for maintenance.

In some countries the legal consequences of adoption do not extend as far as they do in England. In West Germany, for instance, adoption is a civil contract between the child's natural mother and the adopting parents, the terms of which may vary. Sometimes such contracts explicitly exclude the possibility that the child shall inherit anything from the adoptive parents.[33]

Some systems of law make no provision for legal adoption at all. For example, in traditional Muslim law the legitimation of illegitimate people is not possible. There are no legal processes of legitimation and no persons or group with the power to make or declare an illegitimate individual legitimate; the subsequent marriage of parents would not legitimize an illegitimate child, for instance. There are passages in the Koran which, it is argued, outlaw adoption:

> Allah . . . does not regard your divorced wives as your mothers, nor your adopted sons as your sons. These are mere words that you utter with your mouths. . . . Name the sons after their fathers and if you do not know who their fathers are regard them as brothers in the faith and as wards.[34]

However, the traditional Muslim punishments for fornication and adultery must make recognized illegitimacy an extremely rare phenomenon in Islamic states.

Is there in English law any process which can render a legitimate person illegitimate? The only process which had the effect of removing the advantages of legitimacy, it could perhaps be argued, was the now obsolete process of attainder. Under common law attainder was the consequence of sentence of death, the criminal judged not fit to live being called 'attaint' or condemned. The meaning of the word became confused with the idea of taint or stain. Attainder took place after judgment of death or its equivalent (e.g. judgment of outlawry on a capital charge). The consequences of attainder were forfeiture and corruption of the blood, this latter phrase signifying that the attainted person could not inherit anything, nor transmit estates, rights or goods to any heirs. Hence both he and his descendants lost the rights of legitimate people. Henry VIII added to the doctrine of treason and attainder his Treasons Act (1534) and other treason legislation. Later the jurist Coke (1552–1634) described attainder thus:

> Implied in this judgment [i.e., that of treason] is, first, the forfeiture of all his manors, lands tenements, and hereditaments . . . secondly, his wife to lose her dower; thirdly, he shall lose his children, for they become base and ignoble; fourthly, he shall lose his posterity, for his blood is stained and corrupted, and they cannot inherit to him or any other ancestor. . . . and reason is that his body, lands, goods, posterity etc. should be torn, pulled asunder, and destroyed, that intended to tear and destroy the majesty of government.[35]

It was possible for the heirs of attainted men to be restored to their 'lands, goods, posterity etc.' by Act of Parliament: Robert Devereux, the son of that Earl of Essex who was executed for treason by Elizabeth I, was 'restored in blood and honour' by Act of Parliament under James I.

CHAPTER 4

The Custody of Legitimate Children

HISTORY

The general rule in the past was that a legitimate child belonged by law or custom to its father. In ancient times a woman could not be the guardian of her own children – firstly, because she was herself under guardianship of some kind all her life and, second, because quite usually a married woman's right to own property or real estate was either restricted or non-existent, making it difficult or impossible for her to support a child.

In Rome in early times the *paterfamilias* had the right of life and death over his children, wife and slaves. These people did not own property: they *were* property. An unmarried free woman had a guardian, usually her father, or, if he were dead, one of his kinsmen. A married woman's guardian was her husband. Even widows were in guardianship, the guardian being appointed by the state if no suitable kinsman were available. A child born to a woman in slavery did not belong to its mother but to her master. In later periods the right of the *paterfamilias* over the life and death of the members of his family and household was reduced, and in the fourth century it was repressed, although he retained his role of guardian. Under Justinian it became possible for widows to act as guardians of their own children in certain circumstances.[1]

The Anglo-Saxons also held that a woman must have a guardian. Guardianship is the origin of the custom in which a bride's father 'gives her away' to the bridegroom at the wedding ceremony. On the other hand, Anglo-Saxon law allowed a widow to inherit property from her husband in certain cases, for that society assigned definite rights and duties to paternal and maternal kin respectively, so that each side had specific, recognized claims on inherited property. The father's rights over his children were not as extensive as those of the Romans, but some authorities believe that an Anglo-Saxon father was permitted to destroy a new-born child if he did not want to rear it. In England at the end of the Saxon period women gained certain rights and some independence. For example, it became possible for a woman to sue on her own behalf instead of through a guardian, as formerly. A Saxon woman had always had the duty, and possibly always a right of some kind, to look after the person of her own child: its father or paternal kinsmen were responsible for looking after its property.[2]

After the Norman Conquest and throughout the Middle Ages it remained the case that in law the guardian of a child was its father. If the father died, the amount and the type of property which was to be inherited by the child determined the question of who became its guardian. Among the peasantry a wife shared her husband's property, presumably because the quantity was too small to be divided and because the survival of Anglo-Saxon customs connected with the rights of maternal kin lingered on in families of Anglo-Saxon stock. The 'law of the nobles', which was, of course, Norman in origin, was that the property was neither divided nor shared but belonged solely to the husband. The wife's property became the property of the husband on marriage. This 'law of the nobles' pushed aside the common law notions which derived from the Saxons, so that by the end of the Middle Ages the legal capacity of married women to own property had almost disappeared. Common law affirmed a man's duty to support his legitimate children until they were grown up. The father also had a right of custody which was absolute as against the mother. Any action whereby a father attempted to divest himself of the custody of his legitimate children in order to give custody to the mother was void as contrary to public policy. It was not until 1873 that this doctrine of the absolute custody rights of the father was formally abandoned. Custody of the children carried with it certain supplementary rights, such as the right to punish and the right to educate the child. Until 1660 a widow 'inherited' the right of custody from the deceased father, but after that date it became possible for a man to appoint a testamentary guardian whose rights would be the same as those of a living father. A testamentary guardian could remove the child of a widow from its mother's care if he so wished. This remained the law in England until 1886.[3]

In the sixteenth and seventeenth centuries individuals and families sometimes tried to circumvent the general legal incapacity of married a woman to own property by devising special contracts. One method was for the father of a bride to set up a prenuptial contract, the intended effect of which would be to protect the woman's property from being misused or squandered by her husband. Another device was to make a will in such a way that a married daughter could 'have the use of' inherited property during her lifetime, after which it would pass to her husband or sons. Fathers also tried to make wills which postponed the distribution of property until after the death of a son-in-law, so that a married daughter could inherit as a widow. The courts did not always regard such wills and contracts as valid. By the time of Charles II it had become possible in law to settle money on a married woman for her own use, although her husband's permission was needed. This amelioration had no effect on the custody of children.[4]

The inability of married women to own property is a significant premise of the plots of many plays and novels of the seventeenth, eighteenth and nineteenth centuries from the comedies of the Restoration to the stories of Trollope and Henry James.

In 1837, at the beginning of Queen Victoria's reign, the custody of a child was still vested solely in its father. During the 140 years that have elapsed since then three fundamental changes in legal doctrine have occurred.

1. In 1839 a married woman had no right to the custody of her children. By 1971 the rights of a married woman were equal to those of the father. Several major Acts of Parliament were needed to bring about this equalization of parental rights, which to date applies only to legitimate children.

2. During roughly the same period a married woman's legal inability to own property was removed step by step. This too took a great deal of legislation. The first step was the Divorce Bill of 1857.[5] This was followed by a series of Acts called the Married Women's Property Acts. Finally, in 1935 the Law Reform Act[6] placed married women on a footing of equality with other adults in respect of property law.
3. Between 1857 and 1937 a series of laws and amendments to laws have brought about a formal equality between men and women in regard to divorce.

There is a considerable overlapping of subject matter in these three sets of statutes. The divorce Bills contain clauses about the property rights of (ex)-married women; the Married Women's Property Acts have provisions relating to divorced and separated people; and the Custody of Children Acts are concerned, *inter alia*, with the parental rights and duties of spouses who have been separated by death or legal process or any other cause.

The most important of these Acts of Parliament are the following.

Talfourd's Custody of Children Act, 1839[7]

Talfourd's Act enabled a court to give custody of children aged less than seven years to the mother when the parents had separated, and to allow her access to children aged between seven and 21. The fourth paragraph of Talfourd's Act states that no mother who has been judged guilty of adultery can be awarded custody by a court. Adultery by a father has never automatically cancelled his right to custody or access.

Lord Cranworth's Divorce Bill, 1857[8]

Cranworth's Divorce Bill transferred the power to make divorces from the ecclesiastical courts and the House of Lords to the High Court. The divorces that had been granted by the ecclesiastical courts were what would now be called decrees of nullity in some cases or legal separations in others. A decree of nullity allowed remarriage, but a legal separation did not. The House of Lords could grant divorce decrees which allowed remarriage. The grounds were limited: they were adultery by a wife or adultery aggravated by bigamy, incest or unnatural offences by a husband. According to Bromley,[9] there are on record only four cases of wives obtaining divorces from the House of Lords. Lord Cranworth's Bill contained important clauses having to do with property. A deserted wife's earnings could no longer be claimed by her husband but were to be treated as her own. Other provision was made for deserted wives too, by making it possible for them to sue their husbands for maintenance. Separated wives were given the power to sue persons other than their husbands for debt, libel and so on; previously a wife could sue only through her husband.

The Married Women's Property Act, 1870[10]

This first Act concerned specifically with married women's property enabled a married woman to keep her own earnings. Later Acts gradually increased the property rights of a married women and also their duties in so far as these related to property. Thus, for example, the Married Women's Property Act of 1893[11] enabled married women to make contracts and wills, and the Married Women's Property Act of 1908[12] placed on married women certain obligations to help support their own aged parents.

The Custody of Infants Act, 1873[13]

This Act empowered the court to give custody of children up to the age of 16 to the mother. It replaced Talfourd's Act of 1839 and, interestingly, it did not include Talfourd's proviso concerning adulterous mothers. But until the twentieth century the courts continued to treat a mother's adultery as an automatic bar to custody and often also as a reason for forbidding access.

The 1873 Act is especially important because of the following clause:

> No agreement contained in any separation deed made between the father and the mother of an infant or infants shall be held to

> be invalid by reason only of its providing that the father of such an infant or infants shall give up the custody and control thereof to the mother. . . .

(It will be remembered that under common law any attempt by a father to divest himself of the right of custody in favour of the mother was void as contrary to public policy.)

The Judicature Act, 1875[14]

This Act transferred the power to make divorces from the High Court to a specially constituted Divorce Court.

The Custody of Infants Act, 1886[15]

This Act enabled the court to give custody of children to the mother until the children came of age. It also altered the law on testamentary guardianship, so that the powers of a testamentary guardian were no longer absolute against the widowed mother but, other things being equal, had to be shared with her. The Act also gave to widowed mothers some power to appoint testamentary guardians themselves.

The Matrimonial Causes Act, 1923[16]

This Act equalized the legal position of men and women in regard to the possible grounds for divorce by making proven adultery by either party to a marriage a sufficient ground for divorce by the other.

The Guardianship of Infants Act, 1925[17]

This Act equalized the legal position of the father and the mother in respect of the custody of their children. It has been repealed, but the relevant legislation has been incorporated in the Guardianship of Minors Act of 1971 (see below).

The Law Reform (Married Women and Tortfeasors) Act, 1935[18]

This Act finally abolished the separate category of married women's property and gave to married women the same powers and rights in respect to property and the law of property as other adult persons.

A. P. Herbert's Divorce Bill, 1937[19]

This Bill introduced new possible grounds for divorce, namely cruelty, insanity, three years' separation. Each could be a ground either for a wife or for a husband.

The Guardianship of Minors Act, 1971[20]

This Act formally equalizes the legal position of the father and the mother of a legitimate child in respect of guardianship and custody. The gist of the Act is to be seen in the following clause:

> when, in any proceedings before a Court . . . [regarding] (i) the custody or upbringing of a minor, or (ii) the administration of any property belonging to or held in trust for a minor, the Court, in deciding the question, should regard the welfare of the minor as the first and paramount consideration, and shall not take into consideration whether from any point of view the claim of the father, or any right possessed by the father at common law, in respect of such custody, upbringing, administration, or application as superior to that of the mother, or the claim of the mother as superior to that of the father.

CUSTODY AND PROPERTY CAMPAIGNS IN THE NINETEENTH CENTURY

The changes in English law described in the foregoing sections were in several cases the results of public campaigns or agitation by individuals. Many people were involved, women especially. Some of the more famous names are those of Caroline

Norton, Thomas Noon Talfourd, Barbara Bodichon, John Stuart Mill, Dr and Mrs Pankhurst, Professor and Mrs Henry Fawcett, A. P. Herbert.

The first Bill, Serjeant Talfourd's Custody of Infants Act of 1839, came into existence as the direct result of Caroline Norton's struggle to be allowed access to her three children after she and her husband had separated. Lord Cranworth's Divorce Bill of 1857 contained clauses about custody and property the necessity of which had been suggested by the Norton imbroglio, and the same thing is true of the first Married Women's Property Act.

In Sheridan's Play *The Rivals* Mrs Malaprop says: "Tis safest in marriage to begin with a little aversion."[21] This joke rang horribly true for the playwright's granddaughter Caroline and her husband George Norton, who developed a spectacular mutual aversion, to which we owe many works, both of history and of fiction, and several changes in English law.

Sheridan's granddaughters were all considered very beautiful and distinguished, and they all made good marriages (in the conventional sense) in spite of the fact that they lacked dowries. One of them married a duke. Caroline Sheridan married George Norton, the younger brother of Lord Grantly. The Nortons were Tories and the Sheridans were Whigs, and no doubt this political dimension is one of the reasons why the Norton 'case' has interested so many historians and biographers.

It seems that George Norton was quarrelsome and at times violent and that Caroline Norton was strong-willed, not a characteristic much appreciated in nineteenth-century wives. Caroline complained to her family about George's general behaviour; as a result, the Sheridans came to dislike George and he came to dislike them. This unhappy and unfortunate marriage lasted for 12 years, and there were three sons.

In 1831 Caroline Norton met Lord Melbourne, who formed an intense but apparently platonic attachment to her which lasted for many years. The friendship was not clandestine. George Norton knew about it and did not (at first) object to it; indeed, it seems that he obtained some political preferment because of it. It is not at all easy to decide, after more than a century, whether or not Caroline was in love with Melbourne or whether or not adultery was committed by the pair. The evidence – including Caroline's well-known poem 'I Do Not Love Thee' – is ambiguous.

In 1835 Lord Melbourne became Prime Minister.

One day in 1836, probably after a domestic quarrel, Caroline Norton left her house to visit her sister who lived nearby. This visit was soon interrupted by the arrival of one of Caroline's servants, who told her that her three sons were being sent away somewhere by their father. She hastened back to her house, but the children were not there, and George refused to tell her where they were. Eventually she traced them to the house of a Mr Knapp, George's agent. He had locked them up and refused to allow Caroline to see them. He said he would call the police if she did not leave his house. After this incident Caroline did not return home but went to stay with her Sheridan relatives. Newpapers and scandal sheets began to publish stories alleging that she had deserted her husband. Because she was a married woman, it was possible to libel her with impunity, since married women could only sue people via their husbands.

Norton sent the three children to Scotland, to their grandmother, and gave strict instructions that Caroline was not to be allowed to see them. Her lawyers then tried to bring about a reconciliation, but Norton was seeking a divorce and asked his own lawyers to look for evidence of adultery. No such evidence could be found. Norton then brought a suit in law against the Prime Minister, alleging alienation of his wife's affections.

The case of *Norton v. Melbourne* was heard in June 1836. Melbourne's legal advisers were Sir John Campbell and Serjeant Talfourd. The jury, who listened to Norton's witnesses 'with incredulity and disgust',[22] found for Lord Melbourne without leaving the courtroom. As Norton left the building, he was hooted by the crowd. In spite of this defeat Norton continued his war with his wife and continued to refuse her any access to the children. Further attempts by her lawyers at bringing about a reconciliation failed. George Norton's own friends and associates turned against him; one of his lawyers, John Bailey, wrote to Caroline:

> I blush for human nature when I see a woman so cruelly treated by a man, and that man her husband. . . . I was one of the advisers in that hateful trial. . . . I can never repair the injury I have occasioned. . . . I came into this negotiation as Mr Norton's friend and have been forced by a sense of justice to turn my back on him.[23]

It appears that after more fruitless meetings either Caroline or her lawyers or both approached Talfourd, who was MP for Reading, with the suggestion that he present a Bill to Parliament to alter the law on custody. Possibly he was approached via the Prime Minister. Talfourd presented his Custody of Children Act to the House of Commons in 1838; the House of Commons passed it, but it was thrown out by the House of Lords. In 1839 he tried again, this time successfully.

As the Norton children were living in Scotland, this change in English law was at first not much use to their mother. It was not until 1841, when the boys left Scotland to go to school, that Caroline was able to take legal action. She began legal proceedings when the headmaster of the school, acting on Norton's instructions, refused to allow her to visit the boys. Once legal proceedings had been started Norton gave way and stopped obstructing his wife's access to the children. From that time forward she saw them at regular intervals.

Mrs Norton died in 1876. During her lifetime she was quite well-known as an authoress. She published four novels – all of them about love and marriage! – and much poetry. She and her sisters also wrote ballads, some of which are still occasionally sung today, the most popular being 'The Arab's Farewell to His Steed'.[24] She wrote too some political essays about custody and property and women's rights. These essays belong to a body of Victorian literature on women's rights and the legal position of women which includes the monographs on education and property and other matters written in the 1850s and 1860s by Barbara Leigh Smith, and John Stuart Mill's *The Subjection of Women*, and the books, pamphlets and petitions of the suffragists and suffragettes. If we can believe that our rulers respond not only to force but also to the arguments of their subjects, then we can believe that this body of literature did indeed influence law making in England in the nineteenth century and later, and hence influences the way we live now.

One of Caroline Norton's essays dates from 1854 and is called *English Laws for Women in the Nineteenth Century*. In law Caroline Norton's property and earnings belonged to her husband, and even after they had separated he claimed the copyright on all her publications. At the same time he refused to pay her debts. In 1853 there was a court case in which a coachbuilder sued for payment of a bill for repairs to Mrs Norton's coach. She was unable to pay the bill, and her estranged husband was not willing to. He was not under any legal obligation to make her an allowance, although he was the legal owner of her property and earnings. Caroline Norton's own pamphlet on the laws did not create much stir, but a little later Barbara Leigh Smith (Mrs Bodichon), the daughter of a Radical MP, published a similar work called *A Brief Summary in Plain Language of the Most Important Laws Concerning Women*. She also got up a petition to Parliament urging changes in the law. This was signed by over 24,000 people. As a result Sir Erskine Perry, MP for Davenport, introduced a Bill which would have made some of the reforms suggested by Miss Leigh Smith. However, during that year (1857) Lord Cranworth's Divorce Bill was also before the House, and what happened in the end was that some clauses from Erskine Perry's Bill were incorporated in the Divorce Bill.

In the 1860s and 1870s the agitation for reforms in the law of marriage and property was taken over by the Married Women's Property Committee. Dr and Mrs Pankhurst became prominent members of this organization: they were not satisfied with the provisions of the first Married Women's Property Act of 1870 and continued campaigning on the issue for many years. The 1882 Married Women's Property Act was drafted by Dr Pankhurst.[25]

John Stuart Mill was another well-known campaigner on these and related matters. Mill was MP for Westminster between 1865 and 1868, and when the 1867 Reform Bill[26] was passing through the House of Commons he tried to introduce clauses which would have given women the vote. In this, of course, he was not successful. In 1869 he published *The Subjection of Women*. Chapter 2 of this work describes the law of property as it affected married women and contains the following strong passage:

> what is (a wife's) position with regard to the children in which she and her master have a joint interest? They are by law *his* children. He alone has any rights over them. . . . Even after he is dead she is not their legal guardian, unless he by will has made her so. He could even send them away from her, and deprive her of the means of seeing or corresponding with them, until this power was in some degree restricted by Serjeant Talfourd's Act. . . . If she leaves her husband she can take nothing with her, neither her children nor anything which is rightfully her own. . . . only legal separation, by decree of a court . . . entitles . . . her to live apart, without being forced back into the custody of an exasperated jailer – or . . . empowers her to apply any earnings to her own use, without fear that a man whom she has perhaps not seen for 20 years will pounce upon her some day and carry all off.[27]

The legal right of women to own and inherit property, and to use the money which they themselves earn, has grown symbiotically with their legal right to a share in the custody and guardianship of their children. It is obvious why this should be so. On the one hand, the individual who gives birth to a child plainly has as much natural right to its custody as the individual who begets the child; on the other hand, however, there is no point in making this natural right into a legal right if other laws prevent the parent from spending money and owning property, for the rearing of children is a task which requires a considerable amount of money and cannot be undertaken by people who are permanently penniless.

The law is still changing, and so are customs governing family life. Nowadays (1981) judges in England seem to work on the assumption that the mother is the best person to have custody of a child, and more mothers are given custody at divorce than fathers. Changes having to do with social security payments, mortgages and rights in the family home have placed women in a stronger position than formerly. There is some feeling that the pendulum has swung too far – recently an organization called Families need Fathers has been set up whose general aim is to call in question the assumption that mother are the best people to have custody in most cases. Families need Fathers wants a review of the laws now governing custody, access and the distribution of family real estate. An entirely different kind of organization is working for similar aims in Australia. According to a Melbourne newspaper:[28]

> A Melbourne Family Law Court Judge received a death threat at his home last night. . . . The threats follow the murder in Sydney on Tuesday of Mr Justice David Opas, also of the Family Court. . . . (the) President of the Army of Men and Women said . . . there was 'no doubt' that another Family Law Court Judge would be killed. The Army of Men and Women was set up . . . three years ago to oppose the [1975] Family Law Act and the way it is applied in the Family Courts.

CHAPTER 5

The *filius nullius* Rule

In the ancient world the problem of illegitimacy was often dealt with by the simple expedient of destroying the future bastard's mother before the child was born. Questions and difficulties about guardianship, custody and property of illegitimate children do not arise if illegitimate children are fated to die in their mother's wombs.

In biblical times an adulteress was stoned to death.[1] This is also the proper punishment for adultery according to Islamic law. In a polygamous society 'simple bastardy' can be avoided by making a man marry the unbetrothed girl or girls he has intercourse with: this rule is probably quite common. It is stated in Deuteronomy:

> If a man find a damsel that is a virgin . . . and lie with her, and they be found;
>
> Then the man that lay with her shall give unto the damsel's father fifty shekels of silver, and she shall be his wife. . . . he may not put her away all his days.[2]

Adulterine bastardy would be a more difficult problem, but a very powerful man such as a king could, if he wished, arrange to circumvent the usual punishment, as we learn from the story of David and Bathsheba. David saved Bathsheba's life by arranging the death of her husband Uriah in battle and making her his own wife.[3]

In Rome, according to Plutarch,[4] a Vestal Virgin who broke her vow of chastity was ceremoniously buried alive. But death was not a standard punishment in Rome for unchaste women; thus illegitimate children were born, and there were laws relating to their support and status. In Roman law a child born not earlier than the seventh month after the beginning of a marriage and not later than the tenth month after its end was assumed to have been conceived in wedlock and was legitimate unless its mother's husband refused to recognize it. A child born outside those limits was illegitimate. Traditionally, a man recognized the new-born infant by lifting it up in the air, after which the child was irrefutably legitimate. The Romans classified illegitimate children into *nothi* and *spurii*. The first were the children of concubines and had certain legal claims on the father for support. They could be legitimated by the subsequent marriage of their parents. Under Justinian such children could also be legitimated by an Imperial act of grace, provided that the father had no legitimate children already, the mother was a free woman and there was some special reason why the parents could not legitimate the child themselves by marrying. *Spurii* had no claims on the father. Illegitimate children and their mothers generally had rights and duties of support of a reciprocal nature, according to Max Käser,[5] although since a woman could not hold or establish domestic power and had restricted property rights, it is not altogether easy to see how she could fulfil an obligation to support a child. Maternal grandparents had no duty of support in relation to illegitimate children.

Before the invention of wills and testaments estates went by custom to kin, and illegitimate offspring did not count as kin. Later on, the laws governing the making of wills made it difficult for a man to leave an estate to an illegitimate child.

Apart from matters involving support and inheritance, an illegitimate person in Rome suffered few other disabilities. He was allowed to take public office, for example.

It should not be forgotten that the practice of exposing unwanted infants was common in Rome, and it seems safe to assume that many *nothi* (especially females) and perhaps most *spurii* would have been dealt with in this way.

Early Norse law forbade the exposure of infants.[6] It was comparatively easy for a Norse freeman to legitimate an illegitimate son. All he had to do was to adopt the child into his household and start treating it as his own, though he was supposed first to obtain the permission of his heir. Interestingly, modern German law allows a somewhat similar method of legitimation. In West Germany a man can legitimate a natural child by making a legal declaration after obtaining the permission of his wife (if he is married) and of the child's mother. Parental authority over a child legitimated in this way passes from its mother to the father and his wife and is not shared between the father and the mother, as would be the case if the child were born legitimate.[7]

ROYAL AND NOBLE BASTARDS

In theory at least, Christian society has always allowed a bastard child and its mother to live. Often enough, of course, such people have lived and died as outcasts and pariahs, subject to many punishments and much social persecution. On the other hand, the illegitimate children of kings and nobles, if known to be such, could be very well-treated indeed, the power and wealth of the fathers ensuring that the children acquired a kind of quasi-legitimate status.

Einhard tells us that the Emperor Charlemagne kept concubines and had several bastard children, both sons and daughters. One illegitimate son, Drogo, became Bishop of Metz; another, Hugo, was Abbot of St Quentin. A third bastard son

> handsome in face but hunchbacked, named Pepin . . . shammed sickness and plotted against his father with some of the leading Franks, who seduced him with vain promises of the royal authority. When his deceit was discovered, and the conspirators were punished, his head was shaved, and he was suffered, in accordance with his wishes, to devote himself to a religious life in the monastery of Prum.[8]

Among the Germanic tribes in pre-Christian times legitimacy was partly a matter of race and class, so that a child could not be legitimate if its parents were unequal in rank or of different races. (A similar principle is upheld today in South Africa, which, of course, is ruled by people of Dutch descent.) Both before and after the coming of Christianity bastards were debarred from holding public office, but this rule was often ignored by royal and noble fathers and sons. The Frankish Theodoric I, a natural son of the Emperor Clovis, shared the kingdom with his legitimate half-brothers; Arnulf made his natural son, Zwentibold, King of Lorraine in AD 895; William the Conqueror was the illegitimate son of Robert, Duke of Normandy.

In England since the Conquest the surname Fitzroy has sometimes been given to the bastards of kings (Fitz = *fils*). Sometimes, too, kings have named their illegitimate children after themselves, so that the families of England include the Fitzwilliams, the Fitzhenrys, the Fitzjameses and the Fitzcharleses.

According to Anthony Wagner, bastardy has often led to a significant spreading of the royal blood through the community. Of the royal bastards born since the reign of Henry I, about 40 have descendants living today. A good example of this spreading of the royal seed is the following. Henry VII had an illegitimate son called Robert Velville; one of Robert Velville's granddaughters, Catherine Berain, lived in Wales, married three times and had a very large number of children, on account of which fact she was nicknamed *Mam Cymru* (Mother of Wales).[9]

Probably the most notorious begetters of bastards in the royal line of England are Henry I, Henry VII, Henry VIII, Charles II, James II and William IV.

Although William the Conqueror is an ancestor of all English kings, and although the legitimacy of Elizabeth I was rather dubious, bastardy has always been regarded – in theory at least – as barring the way to the throne. In *Henry VI Part I* Shakespeare makes the French nobles refer contemptuously to the English royal line as 'the Bastard Plantagenets'. To argue that a man is illegitimate or is descended from illegitimate ancestors is to argue that he has no right to the throne. But such reasoning does not always convince: in 1485 Richard III issued a proclamation which reads in part as follows:

> the rebels and traitors have chosen to be their captain one Henry Tudor, son of Edmund Tudor, son of Owen Tudor, which of his ambitiousness and insatiable covetousness encroacheth and usurpeth upon himself the name and title of

> royal estate of this realm of England, where unto he hath no manner of interest, right, title, or colour, as every man knoweth; for he is descended of bastard blood both of the father's side and the mother's side, for the said Owen, the grandfather, was bastard born, and his mother was daughter unto John, Duke of Somerset, son of John, Earl of Somerset, son unto Dame Katherine Twyford, and of their double adultery begotten, whereby it evidently appeareth that no title may be his.[10]

This proclamation proved ineffective, however.

Charles II had numerous bastard children and he made six of his bastard sons dukes. Thirteen of his mistresses are known by name.[11] However, his court was very dissolute, both before and after he became king, so it was not always easy to know who had fathered which bastard. For example, one of Charles's mistresses, Lady Castlemaine, married to Roger Palmer, took other lovers as well as Charles but preferred to father her children on the king rather than on Palmer or on other lovers. In his *Diary* Samuel Pepys describes a rumpus involving this lady:

> Fenn tells me that the King and Lady Castlemaine are quite broke off, and she is gone away, and is with child, and swears the King shall own it: and she will have it christened in the Chapel at White Hall so, and owned for the King's as other Kings have done; or she will bring it into the White Hall gallery, and dash the brains of it out before the King's face.[12]

Charles recognized several of Lady Castlemaine's children as his own. . . .

Charles's generosity towards his illegitimate children was quite marked. He always tried to organize advantageous arrangements for these sons and daughters, marrying them off to rich people, conferring titles on them, giving them Crown lands when he could and empowering them to collect taxes on a wide range of items, from coals to wine. Nell Gwyn's son was made Duke of St Albans and given the hereditary title of Master of the Hawks, a sinecure that carried with it an income of £965 per annum; some of his older half-brothers and half-sisters had incomes of many thousands of pounds per annum. Having no legitimate children, Charles must have been tempted to give the name Stuart to one or other of his sons, but he resisted this temptation. If he had not been firm about that, his Parliament would soon have sent him on his travels again.

'THE FATHERLESS POOR MAN'S CHILD'

Most societies distinguish between licit and illicit birth. The distinction comes closest to breaking down when substantial numbers of individuals of both sexes are propertyless and living in slavery or servitude as convicts, 'internal exiles', slaves or other long-term prisoners. Thus, for example, we find His Majesty's Select Committee on Transportation complaining in 1812: 'Two-thirds of the children born each year in the colony of New South Wales are illegitimate.'[13] And in our day Alexander Solzhenitsyn reports the existence of a somewhat similar situation in the 'Gulag Archipelago'. When three-thirds of the children born are 'illegitimate' the distinction between legitimate and illegitimate has evaporated: but there are reasons (discussed below) why this is unlikely to happen even in a very unstable society. Nevertheless, the distinction can be weakened in large sections of a society. Some authorities argue that the prevalence of illegitimacy in the countries of the West Indies can be traced to the influence of the slave trade. The enforced instability of marriages between slaves was convincingly described by Harriet Beecher Stowe in her anti-slavery novel *Uncle Tom's Cabin*.[14] In general, the marriage of persons in bondage has little social point, since such a marriage can easily be nullified in effect, even if not strictly speaking in law, by some third party – the slaves' master, for instance.

During the early Middle Ages marriages between serfs were not regarded as legally binding. A serf did not own his own person, so he could hardly bestow it upon another. Canon law allowed that marriages between serfs need not be legally binding. An eighth-century decree says:

> If a freeman take to wife another man's bondwoman, in the belief that she is a freewoman, and if the woman be afterward convicted of servitude, if he be able to buy her free from servitude, let him do so. . . . if he cannot let him take another wife if he will.[15]

Albertus Magnus defended this decree – not as natural law but as a law of the Church.[16] Hadrian IV, Pope from 1154 to 1159, declared that marriage between serfs must be treated as binding, but he too made an exception for the case in which a freeman married a bondwoman in ignorance of her status.[17]

In general, a serf could not marry without the consent of the lord of the manor, who, before Hadrian's decree, seemingly had the power to declare invalid any marriages between serfs not authorized by himself. Even after Hadrian's decree the lord could charge a fee (called *merchet*)[18] for giving permission to marry and could fine those who omitted to ask for permission. Some historians suggest that the fee and the fines are the basis of the *jus primae noctis* (if it existed) or of the legend (if it did not).

Fornication was a punishable offence: punishments included whipping, incarceration and a fine called *leyrwite*.[19] Continued fornication or non-payment of leyrwite could lead to excommunication,[20] and stubborn excommunicates could be gaoled by the civil authority on the orders of the bishops. People of all ranks and walks of life were excommunicated for fornication (and, of course, for other offences), though some classes were exempt from excommunication. In England, for instance, tenants-in-chief were exempt, as were sheriffs and other royal ministers. Some excommunicates, similarly, were exempt from civil punishments such as gaoling. Records were kept by the dioceses of excommunications and of the requests made by the bishops for the civil punishment of stubborn excommunicates. Thus it is recorded, for example, that in 1407 the Bishop of Exeter requested the incarceration of one Joan Boyle, excommunicated for her refusal to perform penance for the crime of fornication with the eponymous John Rogger, a monk of Modbury, which fornication had continued for years 'publicly and notoriously'. The co-operation of the civil authorities in such matters was carried out, in England, under an ordinance of William the Conqueror dating from 1072. Punishments were inflicted not only on fornicators themselves but also, in certain cases, on those who aided and abetted them. In Normandy, villages that connived at hiding illegitimate births were subject to penalties.

In Tudor times the ecclesiastical courts were nicknamed the

'bawdy courts', and one could be punished for bringing them into disrepute by calling them that.[21]

Legal punishments for fornication as such were finally removed from English statutes in 1836.

THE OLD POOR LAW

According to canon law and the common law of England, a bastard child was *filius nullius* (no one's child). He could make no claims on his parents for support – no one was *obliged* in law to care for him. In practice, of course, as we have already noted, the illegitimate children of the rich and the great would quite probably be cared for by their mothers and maintained by their fathers, almost as if they were legitimate. The will of the widow Margaret Paston, which she made in 1482, includes the following provision: 'Item, I bequeath to Custance, bastard daughter of John Paston, Knyth, when she is 20 years of age, 10 marks.'[22]

In England throughout the Middle Ages there were no general rules about the support of illegitimate children. By custom the children of the rich depended on their relations, while the 'fatherless poor' relied on the charity of the monastic institutions and the municipalities. Monasteries distributed broken meats and sheltered certain helpless people; municipalities handled sums of money – sometimes large sums – given or willed by pious people for the care of the poor. The guilds made payments to the widows and legitimate children of their members. Towns were allowed to raise money for the care of the poor – the 'town's alms'.

During the sixteenth century, according to Sidney and Beatrice Webb:

> It is plain that the movement for taking the task [of caring for the poor] out of the hands of the Church and dealing with it as part of the civil government was common to practically the whole of Europe. It prevailed alike in Catholic countries and in those which adopted the reformed religion. . . .[23]

The earliest English statute concerned with the care of the

poor is Henry VIII's of 1531. This is therefore the first statute of the Old Poor Law.

In 1533 the City of London set about dealing with the problem of destitution. A committee of 24 leading citizens was set up to consider the question. They began by defining three main types of poor, each type being subdivided into three. Here is their list of the nine classes of poor:

1. (i) The Fatherless Poor Man's Child
   (ii) The Blind, Lame or Aged
   (iii) Lepers
2. (iv) Wounded Soldiers
   (v) Decayed Householders
   (vi) The Diseased Poor
3. (vii) The Rioter that Consumeth All
   (vii) The Vagabond that Will Abide in No Place
   (ix) The Idle Person, as the Strumpet and Others.[24]

At about this time Christ's Hospital, now a public school, was founded, on land in London which had formerly belonged to the Grey Friars, specifically for the care of the 'Fatherless Poor Man's Child'.

The theory in London and elsewhere in England under the Tudors was that destitute children, legitimate and illegitimate, should be looked after by the community – that is, fed, reared and trained for some kind work – all at public expense. They were apprenticed, wherever possible, to a trade. The helpless adult poor, it was thought, should be cared for in hospitals or almshouses, and the 'Rioters', 'Vagabonds' and 'Strumpets' were to be punished (for instance, by flogging).

By 1574, it seems, the parishes and boroughs were beginning to feel overburdened by the large numbers of illegitimate children in their care; in that year a statute was framed which enabled justices to issue bastardy orders, these being orders whereby money could be obtained from the putative fathers of bastards and spent by the parish on the care of the children.

The Poor Law legislation that began with the statue of 1531 continued with further statutes of 1563, 1572, 1576, 1579 and 1601. These empowered the municipalities to raise poor rates, to appoint Collectors for the Poor, and Guardians of the Poor, to suppress corrupt practices in the administration of charitable institutions and so on. Although illegitimate children remained, under common law, *filii nullius*, these statutes of Elizabeth I had the effect, in many instances, of turning such infants into 'children of the parish' or 'children of the borough'.

The idea that the poor should be either set to work or else punished for being poor became more ungenerous, perhaps, in its application during the reigns of the Stuarts and later monarchs. In the seventeenth and eighteenth centuries the poorhouses, almshouses and hospitals gave way, terminologically speaking, to houses of industry or workhouses. The parish became a notoriously bad 'parent', apprenticing children to any master who would take them and bribing tradesmen from outside the parish to take the children away. Unmarried pregnant women were hustled from one workhouse to another, each parish trying to make sure that the illegitimate child was not born within its boundaries. After the Industrial Revolution the Guardians of the Poor took to selling batches of children to the factory owners of Yorkshire and Lancashire, who as often as not would then literally work them to death. Destitute infants were never in short supply. According to the Webbs, the large numbers of children of four years old and over who were used to work the new mills were mostly collected from parish workhouses, the biggest supply coming from London and Westminster, from whence they were taken 'as Sir Samuel Romilly put it "in carts like so many negro slaves" in batches of from five to fifty on the same day'.[25]

The workhouse performed a variety of functions. It was a lying-in hospital for unmarried pregnant women; it was an asylum for their children; it took in the aged poor, the blind, the harmlessly insane and those too ill with physical diseases to be able to earn a living. The separation of its functions did not occur until well into the nineteenth century. About half the inmates of a workhouse (it is believed) would be children, the legitimate and illegitimate offspring of destitute people. In 1834, for instance, there were between 40,000 and 50,000 children living in workhouses in England and Wales. The mortality of such children was frightful. In 1760 80 per cent of the infants born in the workhouse or deposited there by their mothers soon after birth died before reaching the age of 12 months. This led to the practice of 'farming out' babies to private institutions and private homes, as described by Charles Dickens in *Oliver Twist*.[26] But it is not known whether more or fewer babies survived as a result. Medical care of the children and other inmates of the workhouses was contracted for by local doctors, usually for low salaries (for example, £12 per annum) but sometimes for high ones (for instance, Liverpool paid some of its workhouse doctors £300 per annum). The doctors were obliged to vaccinate those living in the workhouse and had to attend at the deliveries of babies, another fact recorded in *Oliver Twist*. According to the Webbs, these duties were not conscientiously performed on the whole, and the general medical care of people living in workhouses was shamefully neglected, whatever the emoluments of the medical men.

Until 1816 the Guardians of the Poor had the right to punish people who lived in workhouses more or less as they saw fit. The corporal punishment of children and adults alike was entirely usual. Other punishments included solitary confinement, the wearing of chains and a reduction of food. In 1816 Sir Samuel Romilly introduced a parliamentary Bill which reduced (though it did not abolish) these powers of the Guardians.

The authority to punish the poor extended beyond the workhouse. Guardians could arrest vagabonds and make them work for farmers at harvest time. In seaports they could arrest vagabonds and ship them aboard vessels that needed extra men. They could arrest and detain children found begging. They were allowed to punish unmarried mothers, whether or not the mother and child were in fact chargeable to the poor rates. In Chester in 1762, for example, the Guardians could make unmarried mothers wear a badge and could sentence them to hard labour and whippings. The Guardians at Gloucester gave themselves similar powers: 'Ordered that Ann Wheeler, mother of a base-born child now chargeable to this house, shall receive 50 lashes according to an advertisement sometimes inserted in the *Gloucester Journal* for ye discouragement of bastardy.'[27] A statute of George III empowered the justices to imprison the mother of a bastard child for up to 12 months. It would seem, though, that summary punishments were more usually administered, for in 1834 the Poor Law Commissioners complained that unmarried mothers were rarely imprisoned, and they recommended that this statute be repealed, which it was. In the nineteenth century a natural or Malthusian penalty such as starvation was felt to be more appropriate.

The statute of 1574 which gave justices the power to issue bastardy orders has already been mentioned. One of the duties of the parish officers in the eighteenth and early nineteenth centuries was the collection of allowances demanded under this law from the putative fathers of illegitimate infants. In most, though not all, parishes part of the sum obtained from the father was handed over to the mother, to be spent by her on the care of the child. The New Poor Law of 1834 forbade this practice, which was thought to make life too easy for unmarried mothers (of this more below). The justices were normally willing to make a bastardy order merely at the request of the parish officer. A man was deemed to be the father of an illegitimate child provided only that the mother of the child was prepared to swear on oath that he was. Now, it was better for the parish, and for the mother and child, if it could be established that a rich man rather than a poor man was the father of an infant. Bastardy orders made against poor men were notoriously difficult to enforce; rich men, on the other hand, especially if married, were sometimes willing to pay hush money even when they were innocent of paternity. For these reasons there was a tendency among parish officers to encourage unmarried mothers to commit perjury. These facts are part of the understood background of Henry Fielding's novel *Tom Jones: the History of a Foundling*.[28] In the first chapter of this novel the baby Tom is discovered in the squire's bed, causing intense and widespread speculation about his origins and some anxiety among local middle-class males. Serious cases of blackmail were uncovered in Manchester in the last decade of the eighteenth century. Huge sums of money disappeared after being handed over to parish officers. Beatrice and Sidney Webb, discussing this matter, work themselves into an absurd state of high-mindedness. They conclude that the blackmail and corruption were much less important than 'the revolting premium placed upon female unchastity' by the practice of allowing the mother herself to spend on the child the money obtained from an affiliation order.[29] The attempt under the New Poor Law to do away with this 'revolting premium' had far-reaching consequences for the *filius nullius* rule.

THE NEW POOR LAW

Abuses of the kind described above were among the many matters discussed by His Majesty's Commissioners for Enquiring into the Administration and Practical Operation of the Poor Laws in 1834. Their Report[30] made a number of recommendations relating to bastardy, several of which passed into law. But these new laws caused a great deal of hardship and distress and were so unpopular that many of the provisions were amended in a series of parliamentary Bills passed between 1838 and 1872.[31]

The principal provisions of the New Poor Law of 1834, in so far as these related to illegitimacy, were as follows.

1. All statutes empowering magistrates to imprison unmarried mothers were repealed.
2. Liability for supporting an illegitimate child was placed on the mother. If she was unable to support the child, the liability fell on the parish or borough.
3. A parish or borough could sue a putative father for maintenance, but the child's mother could not.
4. Suits for maintenance of an illegitimate child had to go to Quarter Sessions, a costly and time-consuming process.
5. The mother's word as to the identity of the father of the child had to be corroborated by other evidence.
6. The maintenance payments made by a father were not to exceed the actual costs – presumably the minimum cost – of supporting the infant.
7. No money recovered from the father of an illegitimate child was to be spent on the mother of the child, and no money recovered from the father was to be entrusted to the mother to spend on behalf of the child.

A direct result of these provisions was to force the mother to place the child in the care of other people, usually the workhouse. Perhaps this was the intention, because new workhouses were built expressly to cope with the changes expected from the operation of the New Poor Law; these were called the union workhouses. If the mother was destitute and unable to find work, she could apply independently for admission to the workhouse, in which case she might find herself under the same roof as her child. But normally the new laws ensured the separation of an unmarried mother from her illegitimate infant.

Part of the point of the stringency of the New Poor Law seems to have been to try to check population growth, though this was never mentioned. At least some of His Majesty's Commissioners wanted to discourage improvident marriages as well as illegitimacy. They were of the opinion that affiliation orders encouraged improvident marriages, since a young man, on receiving such an order or knowing of its likelihood, might say to himself, 'If I have to pay up anyway, I may as well marry the girl!' The new law of 1834 also provided that married couples who entered the workhouse were to be kept apart from each other. This provision, which was not finally abolished until the twentieth century, put a brake on the fertility of the poorest of the poor.

The Commissioners seemed to believe that the best – or possibly the only – way to reduce illegitimacy was to subject the unmarried mother to the 'providential' operation of economic forces. It is not clear whether they realized that Providence, especially economic Providence, usually runs in channels cut by laws. At all events, they were concerned to remove from the statute books those regulations which tended to ameliorate the economic plight of the unmarried mother, while adding new regulations that imposed the duty of support upon her. Some men serving on the Commission wanted the fathers of bastards to be absolved from all responsibility whatsoever and opposed the provision that enabled parishes and boroughs to apply to Quarter Sessions for maintenance orders. One such Commissioner said, 'A base-born child should be a burden to its mother, as Providence evidently intended.' However, the other Commissioners, although agreeing that things should be made hard for the mothers of the base-born, decided that if fathers were absolved from all financial responsibility, an increase in rates and taxes would surely follow. So the provision allowing parishes to apply for maintenance orders was in the end adopted.

The statistics of the time are not reliable – the first Registration of Births Act in England dates from 1836[32] – but what evidence there is suggests that the percentage of illegitimate births actually rose in England and Wales after 1834. Among the common people this was explained by reference to the theory that while the New Poor Law discouraged women from fornication, it encouraged men – and men are stronger than women.

ROSE CAREY AND *HABEAS CORPUS*

The case of *R. v. Nash*,[33] heard in 1883, effectively overturned the common law doctrine that an illegitimate child has, in law, no parent by giving a definite legal weight to the natural tie existing between a child and its mother. As has already been noted, married women had no legal rights, even as regards access, until 1839 and did not acquire a full and equal share in the guardianship of their children until 1971. Unmarried mothers had no legal rights at all in regard to their children until 1883. Roughly speaking, it was only when the idea that a mother could be a legal parent had become possible that the idea that an illegitimate child could have a parent became tenable. The significance of *R. v. Nash* is that it allowed for the first time that a mother was entitled to issue a writ of *habeas corpus* in respect of her illegitimate child. The facts of the case were as follows.

In 1875 a girl, Rose Carey, then aged 14, was seduced and became pregnant. A few months later her father turned her out of his house. In May 1876 Rose Carey gave birth to a daughter, whom she placed with foster parents, Mr and Mrs Nash. The Nashes agreed to care for the baby in return for a weekly sum to be paid to them by the mother. Rose Carey found employment, probably as a servant girl, and she made some payments to the foster parents. However, she then fell ill and went into hospital. When she eventually left hospital she became, in the words of the law report, 'the kept mistress of a gentleman'. She then tried to retrieve the child, but the Nashes had grown fond of it and refused to let it go. In 1880, after negotiations with the foster parents had proved fruitless, Rose Carey summoned Nash before the justices for unlawfully detaining the child. The justices dismissed the summons on the ground that the child was *filius nullius*, no one's child, and therefore did not belong to Rose Carey. In 1882 Rose Carey applied for a writ of *habeas corpus*. The application was heard by Mr Justice North, who refused to issue a writ, again because the child was *filius nullius*. The mother then appealed to the divisional court, which on 5 February 1883 reversed Mr Justice North's decision and ordered that *habeas corpus* should issue. Nash then appealed, and the case was heard in the Court of Appeal, Queen's Bench, before Sir George Jessel (Master of the Rolls), Sir Nathaniel Lindley and Sir Charles Bowen.

Nash's lawyer argued, first, that an unmarried mother had no relationship in law with her child and so no right to *habeas corpus*, and he supported this by referring to other cases in which the courts had refused to return illegitimate children to their mothers. Second, he pointed out that Rose Carey was the 'kept mistress of a gentleman' and so was living in sin: 'the character of the mother is such that it cannot be for the child's benefit that it should be given up to her.' However, the Court found against Nash. Here is part of Sir George Jessel's judgment:

> I am of the opinion that the order [for *habeas corpus*] . . . is clearly right. An unfortunate girl was seduced under the age of 15 and had a child – her father turned her out of doors. She placed the child with two poor people whom she intended to pay for maintaining it. . . . Her health failed and she could not continue the payments. She was obliged to go into an infirmary, and on coming out she fell in with a gentleman with whom she lives as a kept mistress. She is therefore living an immoral life. . . . In a reported case Mr Justice Maule is said to have asked whether the mother of an illegitimate child was anything but a stranger to it. I am disposed to think that this was said ironically. . . . There is in such a case a sort of blood relationship, which, though not legal, gives the natural relations a right to the custody of the child. Here the mother does

> not wish the child to be with her but to be placed with her sister, a respectably married woman. . . . the husband is a clerk . . . and is therefore in a station superior to that of the appellants, and how it can be contended that it is for the benefit of the child to remain with the appellants I do not see.

Sir Nathaniel Lindley concurred:

> We cannot interfere with the right of the mother in favour of strangers. There is indeed no legal relationship, but there is a natural one and the affection of the mother must be taken into account in considering what is for the benefit of the child. The right of the mother as against the appellant is to my mind clear.

Sir Charles Bowen also concurred, but his reasoning was different:

> When we consider what is for the child's benefit, the scale is turned by the respectability of the persons with whom it is to be placed.

Rose Carey's success was perhaps rather a touch-and-go affair. Plainly, it did not result entirely from the court's recognition of a natural right. She claimed custody but made it clear that the care and control of the child would be given to her respectable sister. This side-stepped the objection that a woman living in sin is not a fit person to look after a child, but it also meant that it was not absolutely clear whether the court's final decision rested mainly on a judgment about the child's benefit, or mainly on the assertion of the mother's natural right, or equally on both. Anyway, she was lucky to have a sister who was not only willing to take in the child but was of a higher social status than the poor Nashes, and respectable to boot. And she was very fortunate too to have a gentleman friend, for surely it must have been he who paid Rose Carey's legal fees.

MARGARET MCHUGH AND THE RIGHT TO CUSTODY

The case of *Barnardo v. McHugh*[34] was heard in 1891 by the House of Lords. The circumstances were as follows. Margaret Roddy, a Roman Catholic, lived for 20 years with a certain Mr Jones and had by him a son, John James Roddy, also known as

John James Jones. This boy was baptized in a Roman Catholic church in 1882 and re-baptized in a Protestant church in 1884. Until 1886 he lived with his natural parents, but then this mother married a Mr McHugh, and it is not clear what happened to the boy next. However, in 1888 he was found in the street in a destitute condition by a lady described in the law report as 'a district visitor attached to Emmanuel Church'. This lady took John James Roddy to one of Dr Barnardo's homes, which took him in. The home then got in touch with his mother and asked her to sign an agreement to leave her son in Barnardo's care until he was 21 years of age. Mrs McHugh signed. Some time later she wanted to visit her son at the home, but the managers would not allow her to see him and refused to tell her where he was. Mrs McHugh then wrote direct to Dr Barnardo, asking him to return the boy to her or, alternatively, to hand him over to a male guardian to be nominated by her. Barnardo refused, and there was a correspondence which went on for some time. Barnardo's letters were subsequently described by Lord Halsbury in the House of Lords as 'flippant'.[35] Mrs McHugh applied for a writ of *habeas corpus* and this was issued. She also applied for an order for guardianship, nominating a certain Mr Walsh, a Roman Catholic, as guardian. This order was also made. Barnardo then appealed, and the case eventually went to the House of Lords.

The House of Lords considered several questions in some detail. These questions included the following. Does the mother of an illegitimate child have the same rights of custody and guardianship in respect of her child as those of the father of a legitimate child in respect of his child? If not, what are her rights of custody and guardianship, if any? What rights of custody and guardianship are held by the husband of the mother of an illegitimate child (in this case Mr McHugh)?

The question of whether the mother's former common-law husband (Jones), the natural father of the boy, had any rights of custody or guardianship was alluded to only in passing, the answer to the question being negative under the law as it then stood.

Barnardo's counsel argued that the mother of an illegitimate child had no custodial rights, on the ground that an illegitimate child is *filius nullius*.

The McHughs' counsel argued that the mother of an illegitimate child must have the same rights as the father of a legitimate child: but even if she did not, he said, she must have some right of custody because, according to the Poor Law reforms of 1834, the mother of an illegitimate child had a legal duty to support the child, and such a duty must entail a right to the custody of the child. Finally, he argued, a man had a legal duty to support the children already born of the woman he married; hence Mr McHugh had a legal duty to support John James Roddy and a consequent right to the custody of John James Roddy.

The House of Lords found for the McHughs. Lord Halsbury ruled that the written agreement between Barnardo and Mrs McHugh could not be permitted to pre-empt the question of who was the legal guardian of the child; such an agreement would certainly be null and void if made by and with the father of a legitimate child. Lord Halsbury also reminded the House of Lords of the case of *R. v. Nash.* He was impressed by the references to the New Poor Law, which, he agreed, had placed definite legal obligations on the mother of an illegitimate child, 'which ought, and in my opinion do, bring with them corresponding rights'.

Lord Herschel, concurring on the main issue, said that he did not feel satisfied that the rights of the mother of an illegitimate child had been shown to be the same as those of the father of a legitimate child. But Poor Law legislation 'renders it impossible in the present day to regard the mother of an illegitimate child as destitute of any rights in relation to custody'. Lord Herschel added that the court would not feel bound to accede to the wishes of the mother if it could be shown that it would be detrimental to the best interests of the child for the mother to have custody. Barnardo, who was hostile to Roman Catholicism, had argued that it would be detrimental to the boy's interests to have him change his religion: in the home John James Roddy had been receiving a Protestant religious education. Mrs McHugh's counsel, on the other hand, had argued that the mother had a right to decide what religion the boy was to be brought up in. The court ruled that she had some right 'in the circumstances', but not an absolute right.

ELIZABETH HUMPHRIES AND THE DUTY OF CARE

The case of *Humphries v. Polak* was heard in 1901 in the Court of Appeal (King's Bench).[36] The circumstances were as follows.

In July 1900 Elizabeth Humphries, the mother of an illegitimate daughter, placed this child with a Mr and Mrs Polak for a trial period of one month, and it was agreed that if the foster parents liked the child they would keep it and maintain it thenceforth. When the trial period was over the Polaks reported that they did like the child, and they expressed their willingness to support it from then on. But in November 1900 – that is to say, about three months later – the Polaks changed their minds and wrote to the child's mother to tell her this. They refused to maintain the child any longer. The mother then sued the foster parents for breach of contract. (It should perhaps be noted at this point that modern law governing the adoption of children in England dates from 1926.)

The court found for the Polaks. It opined that the Poor Law reforms of 1834 had placed a legal duty on the mother of an illegitimate child, and it ruled that a mother could not divest herself of her legal duty by contract.

RE D, AN INFANT[37]

There is some disagreement among authorities over the issue of whether adoption completely legitimizes an illegitimate child. The Adoption Acts of 1926,[38] 1950[39] and 1958[40] give to an adopted child in England rights in respect of its adoptive parents which exactly parallel the rights held by a legitimate child against its parents. Such a child is supposed in law to be treated exactly as if it were the legitimate offspring of the adopters. But some lawyers still ask: is it legitimate *really*? Presumably, jurists of a positivistic cast of mind regard the question as nonsensically metaphysical. Bromley says that the status of a child born illegitimate and legally adopted is 'quasi-legitimate'.[41]

In the case about to be described one judge refused to allow an unmarried mother to adopt her own child on the ground that to permit such adoptions would be to destroy the distinction between legitimacy and illegitimacy. The 1950 Adoption Act states: 'An adoption order may be made authorizing the adoption of an infant by the father or the mother of the infant either alone or jointly with his or her spouse.' The same Act makes rules for affiliation orders, and one of these rules says that no affiliation order may be made against a putative father in favour of an adoptive parent *unless the adoptive parent is the child's natural mother*. It seems clear, therefore, that the Act permits the legal adoption of an illegitimate child by its own mother. However, at least two cases had arisen in which a county court judge had queried the intention of the Act and had refused to grant an adoption order to the mother of an illegitimate child. One such decision was successfully appealed against in 1956: this case was heard *in camera*. An appeal against a similar refusal in 1958 was also successful: this appeal was reported, the details being as follows.

The mother of an illegitimate daughter, D, applied for an adoption order, to be made in her own favour, under the Adoption Act of 1950. The application was supported by the Children's Officer of the local authority as guardian *ad litem*. This officer's report reads in part as follows:

> The female applicant is employed as a housekeeper by a Miss R. . . . . the house is modern, comfortably furnished and clean. The infant is at present sleeping in a cot in her mother's bedroom; an adjacent room is available for her use later. The applicant enjoys good health and there is no known history of hereditary disease. She is anxious to remove the stigma of illegitimacy from the child. . . . the care bestowed on the infant is satisfactory and as an adoption order would appear to be in the best interests of the infant it is recommended that an order be made.

The county court judge refused to make an order. In his view, he said, the 1950 Act was not intended to be used for the purpose of removing the stigma of illegitimacy, and the removal of stigma was not a sufficient reason for, nor an advantage to be gained from, the proposed adoption. Surely, he argued, it could not be anything but contrary to the public interest to make it easier to remove the stigma of illegitimacy –

especially if unmarried mothers were themselves permitted to remove the stigma by adopting their own infants! (In this, incidentally, he was upholding a very widespread social rule, namely, the rule that *only a man can legitimate a child.*) The judge said: 'An adoption order, if granted in this case, would no doubt become common form and illegitimacy would automatically be abolished in this country.' Since it could not conceivably be the intention of the 1950 Act to grant 'universal legitimacy', he argued, he could not grant the adoption order to D's mother.

The mother appealed, and the appeal was heard before Lord Denning in 1959. Counsel for the mother argued, first, that the 1950 Act was intended to cover the kind of case in hand; second, that the adoption order entailed advantages over and above the removal of stigma – in particular, advantages having to do with the law regarding inheritance; third, that 13 similar adoption orders had been made by various county court judges in the London area between 1953 and 1959; fourth, that the Appeal Court itself, when sitting *in camera* in 1956, had allowed a similar appeal by a mother against a similar refusal to make an adoption order.

The Appeal Court found for the mother. Lord Denning noted that the natural father was a married man living with his wife (so that legitimation by subsequent marriage was ruled out), and that the mother had never tried to make him financially responsible for the child. She had secure employment and was able to support the child by herself. Her employer was a reasonably wealthy woman, who took an interest in the welfare of the mother and child. Lord Denning decided that these things showed that the mother was a fit person to care for the child and to have custody of it, and was likely to continue to be so. As to the intention of the Adoption Act of 1950, he said:

> it is plain to my mind that the Adoption Act of 1950 contemplates an adoption order being made in the circumstances now before the Court. Section 1(3) and section 2(1) seem to me to contemplate this very case. . . . The Judge seemed to think that by making an adoption order a child is rendered legitimate. That is not the case. Illegitimacy and adoption are entirely different matters. The child still remains illegitimate but being

> adopted it becomes in law for all purposes the child of its mother and suffers none of the disabilities which attach to illegitimacy.

Lord Denning went on to insist that, nevertheless, the natural mother should have no special advantages in law over other potential adopters:

> There must always be an enquiry, of course, whether the mother is a suitable person to be given an adoption order and whether the home is suitable.

This point illustrates one of the main differences between the rights of the father of a legitimate child and the rights of the mother of an illegitimate child. The parental rights of the father of a legitimate child do not depend on his first showing that he is a fit person to have custody of a child; the onus of proof is on those who would show that he is *not* suitable. Although unmarried mothers are now customarily permitted and encouraged to keep their children when they are born, in cases of dipute it would seem that in law the onus of proof lies upon the mother to show that she is at least as suitable a person to adopt as another potential adopter. By definition, this cannot arise in the case of the father of a legitimate child, since he legitimizes the child not by adopting it but by marrying its mother or by being already married to her.

Lord Hailsham's opinion is:

> The extent of her [the unmarried mother's] rights and obligation is open to doubt and it cannot be taken as established that they are the same as those of the father of a legitimate child. . . . the mother has a right [however] to custody and the protection of *habeas corpus*.

Lord Hailsham adds: 'The *filius nullius* rule is now obsolete.'[42]

CHAPTER 6

Marriage

In this chapter and the following one I examine the logical relations between the ideas of kinship, marriage, descent and lineage on the one hand, and the ideas of legitimacy and illegitimacy on the other.

Two main lines of enquiry suggest themselves. These are, first, the question of what the logical relationship is between the idea of marriage and the ideas of legitimacy and illegitimacy; second, what the relationships are between the ideas of family, kinship and descent, and between the ideas of legitimacy and illegitimacy.

Could there be a world in which everyone was legitimate? In a would of very virtuous people or a world with savage customs, such as the stoning of adulteresses and the killing of illegitimate infants – in worlds like these there need be no actual illegitimacy, yet such worlds could articulate the concept, the idea, of illegitimacy.

Could there be a world in which everyone was illegitimate? Surely this could only be the case if there had been an institution of, or like, marriage, which had recently been given up or somehow lost. Among cats there is no marrying or giving in marriage, and there never has been; for that reason, kittens are neither illegitimate nor legitimate. The same would be true of human beings if there never had been any such thing as an institution of, or like wedlock.

Let us now ask two questions. First, is marriage the only institution which does or can generate the concepts of legitimacy and illegitimancy – is marriage a *necessary* condition for the existence of these ideas? Second, does every variety of marriage create the distinction? Is marriage – or any institution that we would call by that name – a *sufficient* condition for the existence of these concepts?

DOES MARRIAGE CREATE THE DISTINCTION BETWEEN LEGITIMACY AND ILLEGITIMACY?

In our society the institution which we call marriage has four main functions or characteristics.

1. Marriage sanctions sexual intercourse. This is probably the aspect which strikes the marriage partners as most important, at least to start with. Emphasis on this aspect of marriage has (in the USA) led homosexuals to demand the right to 'marry' each other.
2. Marriage sanctions reproduction. The children of married partners are legitimate; their existence is sanctioned, correct. They belong to a family and to a lineage, and they are generally entitled to bear a name which shows which family and lineage they belong to.
3. Marriage is an economic and domestic arrangement designed for the support and maintenance of children.
4. Marriage is an economic and domestic arrangement – in fact, a mutual-support system – designed for the maintenance of the marriage partners themselves. Its most notable feature, when regarded from this point of view, is division of labour.

Virtually all the peoples of the world have institutions which combine at least two or three of the above functions under a unified set of rules, and in most societies, probably, all four functions would in fact be combined in one institution. Nevertheless, there is considerable variation in marriage customs. Thus the expression 'marriage partners' may mean a monogamous couple or a polygynous or polyandrous group. Second, different societies have different methods of tracing lineage. This may mean that in some places a child can be legitimate even though it is known that only one of the marriage partners is a parent. For instance, in certain African communities all the children of a married woman count as the legitimate children of her husband, even those who are known to be the results of her adultery with another man. Finally, the economic and domestic arrangements for the support of the children and of the marriage partners vary a great deal between different nations. They vary considerably too within any complex modern society such as our own.

More puzzling than these differences are social institutions which separate the four main functions of marriage (as we understand the institution). If a social institution combines say two or three of the functions listed above, is it marriage or isn't it?

In England a household consisting of a maiden lady and a child which she has adopted and to which she has given her surname is a socially recognized (though rare) type of family group, and it fulfils two of the functions of marriage: child support and legitimation. However this is not marriage. Marriage requires at least two adults.

But what kind of adults? E. E. Evans-Pritchard reports[1] that among the Nuer people of the Sudan women sometimes 'marry' dead men. He calls this 'ghost marriage' and claims that it is quite common. In ghost marriage a living man marries a woman as it were on behalf of a dead man. The living man begets children and has to support them, but they take the name of the dead man, and they belong to the dead man's lineage. The rules of inheritance and other social rules apply to the children as if they were the offspring of the dead man. They are the legitimate offspring of a ghost! Is this marriage? Well, it strikes me as a form of polyandry – a very peculiar form of polyandry, mind you. But if we think of it in that light, it can, I think, be seen to be fulfilling all the main functions of marriage, so surely, therefore, it *is* marriage.

Evans-Pritchard also says[2] that the Nuer have another rather strange kind of marriage, which he calls 'woman marriage'. The partners of a woman marriage are two women who 'marry' each other in an ordinary Nuer marriage ceremony. One of them then takes on the economic role of a (male) husband, which has to do with the cattle, while the 'wife' works at wifely tasks. The 'husband' invites relatives or neighbours to beget children for her on her 'wife'. The males who beget the children are not regarded as partners to a polyandrous marriage. Their status seems to be not unlike that of artificial insemination donors in our own society – except, of course, that the Nuer men are natural insemination donors. Since the children are the legitimate children of the marriage, they take the name of the 'husband' and count as belonging to her kin-group and lineage. When the daughters marry, she collects the bride-wealth of cattle as if she were the (male) husband of their mother. She also has uncle's rights in respect of her nieces.

In these examples the functions of marriage, or marriage as we understand it, have been split up in a strange way. Evans-Pritchard claims that the Nuer call these unions marriage – i.e., they have just one word which applies to ghost marriages, to woman marriages and to marriage between living men and women. Whether we would call woman marriages marriage properly speaking seems in the end to turn into a verbal decision. According to our definition of marriage, a Nuer woman marriage is undoubtedly a borderline case.

All societies which understand the biology of procreation, and which make a distinction between permitted and forbidden sexual union must share a common, though minimal, notion of illegitimacy, which might be expressed thus: *an illegitimate child is one whose existence is the result of an unsanctioned sexual act.* Since virtually all human societies have a ban on incest and most have many other sexual restrictions as well, this minimal notion of illegitimacy must exist in the consciousness of virtually all peoples.

From the fact that the children of a forbidden sexual union are illegitimate it does not follow that the children of a sanctioned sexual union must necessarily be legitimate. For sexual union may be sanctioned in circumstances in which procreation is forbidden. For instance, in our own society today young people are permitted a great deal of sexual freedom, but that does not entail a freedom to reproduce. Unmarried couples are expected and exhorted to take special care about contraception; if pregnancy occurs, they are supposed to arrange either a wedding or an abortion. Those who disregard the rules are thought of as very irresponsible. Again, sexual union may be sanctioned under the rules of institutions designed to cheer up tired businessmen (*Geisha*) or according to specifications which lay down the regulations for the proper conduct of orgies (e.g., those of the Areoi),[3] but such institutions and such regulations do not legitimize children. The children born as the result of Areoi orgies were destroyed at birth. Even a sexual union which is sanctioned for the purpose of begetting and rearing children does not necessarily sanction fertility without limit. In China today married couples are discouraged from having more than one or two children, and there is a new code for punishing couples who have more than this quota. In India recently it was suggested that the fifth, sixth and later children of a married couple should count as illegitimate.

Thus, a legitimate child should be defined as one born as the result not of any sanctioned sexual act but of a sexual act which is sanctioned precisely because it accords with the rules governing reproduction. From this we can derive a slightly more exact definition of illegitimacy, as follows: *an illegitimate child is a child whose conception and birth did not conform to the institutional rules which, in its parents' community, govern reproduction*. These institutional rules, by and large, are what constitute marriage.

So is marriage a *necessary* condition for the existence of the distinction between legitimacy and illegitimacy? The distinction derives from institutional rules governing sexuality, reproduction and fertility, and the care of children. In most societies the sets of rules governing those matters go together, forming unitary institutions which are properly called varieties of marriage. But in some societies the sets of rules are not closely united, so that socially sanctioned unions can exist which fulfil some, but not all, of the functions of marriage, as we understand that term. One function that a 'borderline case' of marriage might well fulfil is the legitimizing of children. Other institutions, such as adoption, also legitimize children, yet are not marriage at all. Hence marriage is not, strictly speaking, a *necessary* condition either for the legitimizing of children or for the generation of a distinction between legitimacy and illegitimacy. But that marriage institutions are the normal and, as it were, paradigmatic preconditions for the generation of the conceptual distinction between legitimacy and illegitimacy can hardly be denied.

IS MARRIAGE A SUFFICIENT CONDITION FOR THE EXISTENCE OF THIS DISTINCTION?

It is logically possible, surely, that there might be a people with an institution that fulfilled all or most of the functions of marriage as we understand the term, but whose lives were such that they had, as it were, no use for the distinction, no use for the notions of legitimacy and illegitimacy. The Eskimo of Baffin Bay might provide an example. The Eskimo of Baffin Bay had a ban on incest (of which they did not always take much heed), so they must have had some notion of a child born as the result of an unsanctioned sexual act – the minimal notion of illegitimacy. But the marriage customs of this people were such that it is hard to see how the minimal notion of illegitimacy could have connected with ideas about extra-marital sexual union. Indeed, although the Eskimo had an institution that was something like marriage, it was so elastic that it is not easy to see what could have counted as *extra*-marital sexual activity.[4] No formal ceremonies marked a marriage. Sometimes two sets of parents would promise their children in marriage, but such promises were not an essential preliminary to a marriage, nor were they regarded as especially binding. When a young man had learned how to support himself by hunting and fishing – usually when he was about 20 – he took a wife, if there were any girls available. Girls left the parental igloo at about 14 in order to live with a husband. There were no premarital bastards because before marriage girls were too young to have children. Female infanticide was practised on a large scale. Scandinavian explorers such as Rasmussen, who visited the area in the 1920s, report that in the settlements visited there were two men to every one woman, in spite of the high mortality rate of adult males that was the result of accidents such as drowning or freezing while hunting.[5] It is believed, therefore, that between 30 and 50 per cent of female infants must have been destroyed at birth. The resulting shortage of adult women led to forms of sexual behaviour (both sanctioned and unsanctioned) which must have made it very difficult to employ a definition of legitimacy and illegitimacy that was based mainly on marriage. There were no formalities of marriage to help distinguish those who were properly married from those who were not, and there were no formalities for dissolving marriages either. If a woman did not get on well with her husband, she could leave him without too much difficulty and would soon find another. Thus although most unions lasted for several years, none was really permanent. The Eskimo also practised wife sharing, wife swapping and wife lending. In spite of these safety valves, attempted rape was common, and wife stealing, sometimes accompanied by husband murder, was not unknown. Robert O'Flaherty's celebrated documentary film *Nanook of the North* shows a polygynous igloo; polygyny was practised by good hunters who could support two wives. But polyandry in some form or other was more common for obvious reasons. As well as a married couple and 'their' children, some igloos contained a young, unrelated man who bore the title 'second husband'. The second husband was a bachelor waiting to find a bride. Because of the shortage of women, he often had to wait a long time, and he was allowed, in the interim, to share an older man's wife.

It seems very probable that for a people with the customs described above, the distinction between legitimacy and illegitimacy could not have had much importance. Of course, the fact that an idea has little importance does not mean that it has no place at all in a people's thought. We make a distinction in our thought between prenuptial and postnuptial legitimate children – since all Western definitions of legitimacy allow such a distinction – in spite of the fact that this distinction has no very important consequences for us. (Considering the intense interest that is usually taken in sexual matters, the gossip that surrounds prenuptial conceptions of legitimate children is surprisingly short-lived.) It seems probable that for some peoples, the Eskimo perhaps included, the distinction between legitimacy and illegitimacy, if it exists at all, can have no more importance than the distinction between prenuptial and postnuptial legitimate child has for us.

It is worth noting, I think, that the Baffin Bay Eskimo, a hunting people, had no real estate and no idea of land as private property. Their movable belongings were their only possessions, and these, out of necessity, were kept to a minimum, as much as could be packed onto a dog sled. The family belongings were the man's hunting weapons, the oil lamp, the woman's sewing implements and the bedding. Security depended not on property but on other people, for a man alone or a couple alone could not survive in the Arctic.

The Eskimo were conscious of living kin and of kinship links. They knew who was related by blood to whom, and they could keep track of kin. But they did not trace lineage back into the past for more than a generation or two. Their idea of illegitimacy could not have been much like ours, for ours is bound up with ideas about property, inheritance, domicile, lineage, naming, marriage and marriage portions, and dowries.

Is the existence of the institution of marriage a *sufficient* condition for the existence of a distinction between legitimate and illegitimate? This depends partly on what is to count as an example of the institution of marriage. As we have seen, some peoples, such as the Eskimo, have mating customs which fulfil the main procreative and child-supporting functions of marriage, as we understand that term, but seem very informal when compared to the procreative arrangements of other peoples. If arrangements like those of the Eskimo are to count as marriage, then it can be argued, I think, that marriage is not, strictly speaking, a *sufficient* condition of the existence of the concepts of legitimacy and illegitimacy. But it could also be argued, of course, that very informal procreative arrangements ought not really to be counted as marriage.

A definition of marriage which links it with legitimacy might run as follows: *Marriage is a relationship between a man and a woman such that the children born to the woman are recognized as the legitimate offspring of both parents.* The anthropologist Kathleen Gough suggests the following amendment:

> Marriage is a relationship established between a woman and one or more men which provides that a child born to the woman in circumstances not prohibited by the rules of the relationship is awarded the full birth-rights common to normal members of his society and social status.[6]

This definition allows for the possibilities of monogamous, polygynous and polyandrous marriage; it covers the widely varying arrangements that human beings make for the care of children; and it covers those marriage customs which are so flexible that they make illegitimacy very rare or so rigid that they make illegitimacy (at least potentially) very common. The definition does not claim that marriage alone can create the legitimacy of an individual; it thus allows for legitimation by means of adoption, for example, or the king's grace. It does not claim that the existence of marriage customs is sufficient to generate the legitimate/illegitimate distinction, since it allows for the possibility that in some circumstances other rules might also be needed. (It is conceivable that such rules might be either subsidiary to the main marriage rules or extraneous to them.)

To sum up: the existence of the legitimacy/illegitimacy distinction is generated by the existence of rules which regulate human reproduction. The rules which generate the distinction form systems of social arrangements which, in general, link sexuality, reproduction, lineage and naming, and inheritance. These systems are called marriage customs or marriage laws. In some societies such systems are very flexible, rudimentary or fragmented by social upheaval: this means that there exists the possibility of border-line cases (cases that are peripheral to the institution of marriage as we understand it). There exists also the logical possibility that human beings might one day be created in laboratories; in that case the link between rules governing sexuality and those governing reproduction would be completely severed, and the rules linking reproduction, lineage and inheritance might also then be altered in unforseeable ways.

No doubt there would be regulations governing the production of test-tube babies, and no doubt the existence of a system of regulations would generate the notion of 'a child (or kind of child) which ought not to be produced'. Furthermore, it is logically possible, of course, that laboratory technicians and others would use the word 'illegitimacy' as a label for that notion. But it is a moot point whether the notion would be the same as, or even similar to, our present notion of illegitimacy. How close it came to ours would depend largely on the basis of the distinction made between the type of child that should be produced and the type that should not – on whether the distinction rested mainly on eugenic considerations, or on considerations having to do with the overall size of the population, or on factors like inheritance and property.

Thus for various reasons we cannot say that marriage is an absolutely *necessary* condition for the existence of the legitimate/illegitimate distinction; nor can we say that it is a *sufficient* condition of it. Nevertheless, marriage, in a broadish sense of the word, is indeed what generates the distinction.

Given the existence of the distinction, marriage is neither necessary nor sufficient to guarantee the legitimacy of the individual, as can be seen from the examples given above. For on the one hand the child of unmarried parents can be legitimized, in at least some societies, by adoption, or by the king's grace, or by other means; and on the other hand – though this is, so far, much more unusual – the child of properly married parents can be declared illegitimate, as, for example, by process of attainder under treason laws or, as was recently suggested in India, as a way of discouraging married couples from having too many children.

CHAPTER 7

Family

The notions of legitimacy and illegitimacy relate to those of family, kinship, blood and descent.

FAMILY

There are different kinds of family, and the word 'family' can apply to more than one kind of group.

When politicians and religious leaders anywhere speak about a need to defend and protect the family and family life they are generally inspired, first, by a wish to protect or strengthen the institution of marriage (e.g., by discouraging divorce, or taxing single people, or punishing fornication or whatever) and, second, by a wish to protect and strengthen parents' rights and powers to control the education and general lifestyle of their own children.

In most Western countries nowadays, it is said, people usually understand by the term 'family' a two-generation group consisting of a married couple and their natural or adopted children – the so-called nuclear family. The nuclear family is often contrasted with the extended family, a kin-group of two, three or even more generations, containing (possibly) grandparents, aunts and uncles, cousins and even, perhaps, more distant relatives still. The potential membership of an extended family will be different in different societies and depends in part on the financial and residential arrangements of the nation, tribe, clan or class, as the case may be. The actual membership of an extended family will partly depend, of course, on who is still alive. In many Western countries what would be the extended family is frequently scattered geographically, but in simpler societies most members of an extended family might well live in one village, or on one estate, or even under one roof. On the other side of the nuclear family is the one-parent family, which, being smaller, could perhaps be named the 'protonic' or 'neutronic' family.

Generally speaking, the term, 'family' refers to a group of people, some of whom are related by blood and some 'in law', containing two or more generations; but the survivors of such a group can also be called a family, especially if they continue to live together in the same house. Thus an elderly couple whose children have left home might be called 'the family' by those children, and a collection of unmarried brothers and sisters living together in their deceased parents' home would also be called a family by many people.

A family can contain people related neither by blood nor 'in law', e.g. children who have been informally adopted or certain old servants such as nannies. At the furthest extreme it is possible for a group of unrelated people – friends, or colleagues, or housemates – to call themselves a 'family' (e.g. the Manson 'family', the Mafia, etc.), but this use is metaphorical, as is the expression the 'family of Man'.

Reference to blood ties and in-laws serves to distinguish (non-metaphorical) families from mere households. A family living together is a household, but not all households are families. A group of blood relatives living under one roof will probably count as a family in the eyes of many people, though if there is only one generation, and if the relationship is not very close, this kind of family is rather a borderline case. Thus, for example, three cousins of the same sex sharing a house is a fairly borderline case of a family, though if they have been brought up together in that very house, it is less borderline and more of a 'real family' than if they were to pool their resources as adults and take a house together.

Unrelated people living together do not count as a real family (even if they have sexual relations with each other) unless, of course, they are tied by marriage, or look as if they are (*de facto* married couples), or have children whom they support, or are about to have a child. Otherwise groups of hotel guests would count as families.

A family is not just any collection of people linked by blood ties. It is a social unit based on (some) blood ties. For, on the one hand, not all blood ties count in delineating a family and, on the other hand, the members of a family can be related to each other 'in law' instead of by blood. Blood ties, biological links, are far too extensive to form the sole basis of a social unit which excludes as well as includes. It could be the case, in a small nation, that everyone is related biologically to everyone else. To be related biologically to someone is not the same thing as being a member of his family. The family – and this signifies the extended family as well as the nuclear family – has rules of inclusion and exclusion which are not purely biological in character. The point of such rules is, in part, to determine who does and who does not have a rightful claim on the material and other resources produced by, or found by, the group; without such rules no limit could be placed on claims. For if *anyone* could make a claim on a group, the group itself would disintegrate. Since long-range planning is an essential ingredient in human society and is impossible unless people can act in groups, the destruction of the family unit (if that were possible) would have to be followed by the creation of other groups which did the same jobs. Such groups would have their own rules of inclusion and exclusion for the reason that the very existence of a social unit with a function depends on their being such rules. No family, commune, *kibbutz*, boarding school or children's home can be all things to all men, though each can do some things for some people.

The American sociologist Kingsley Davis says this about the family and illegitimacy:

> The function of reproduction can only be carried out in a socially useful manner if it is performed in conformity with institutional patterns, because only by means of an institutional system can individuals be organized and taught to cooperate in the performance of those long-range functions [i.e., rearing and educating children], and the function integrated with other social functions. . . . familial institutions constitute the social machinery in terms of which the creation of new members of society is supposed to take place.[1]

Davis further claims that the 'institutional patterns' must of necessity take such a form (or forms) that the rightness of a birth depends on the rightness of paternity:

> the legitimacy rule prevails no matter what other conditions prevail. Children may be an asset or a liability; prenuptial or extranuptial intercourse may be forbidden or sanctioned; still the rule runs that a father is indispensable for the full social status of the child and its mother. Otherwise the child is illegitimate and the mother is disesteemed.[2]

Kingsley Davis is here paraphrasing Malinowski's Principle of Legitimacy, which Malinowski himself states as follows:

> No child shall be brought into the world without a man, and one man, assuming the role of sociological father, that is, a guardian and protector, the male link between a child and the rest of the community.[3]

Before turning to the contentious question of whether Malinowski's Principle of Legitimacy is actually true it will be useful to look at the distinction he draws between the 'biological father' and the 'sociological father'. This distinction would appear to be applicable in any society. In an avunculate family structure, such as that of the Trobriand Islanders (described by Malinowski himself), the sociological father of a child, its guardian and protector, is its biological uncle, i.e. its mother's brother. In our society, of course, the biological father and the sociological father are normally presumed to be one and the same person, but there are plenty of exceptions, both sanctioned and unsanctioned. The sanctioned exceptions include formal and informal adoption (for instance, legal adoption of an unrelated child, informal adoption of a wife's child by a former marriage, adoption of a wife's illegitimate child), and AID with the husband's permission. Thus the class of sociological fathers who are not also biological fathers is by no means empty even in a monogamous society.

A child cannot have more than one biological father, but it is surely *logically* possible for it to have more than one sociological father. Now, if every human society everywhere insisted that for a child to be legitimate it must have at least one, and at most one, sociological father – that is to say, at least one and at most one recognized male guardian – then that would be an interesting fact about the human race. But it is not required by the logic of the concept of the family; nor is it required, in my view, by the logic of the concept of legitimacy. For it is not actually true in all societies that a child can only be legitimate if it has one, and only one, sociological father. It is closer to the truth to say that at least one, and at most one, sociological father is needed to confer legitimacy on a new-born child. For:

1. in polyandrous societies paternity is uncertain, and it can happen, therefore, that the economic responsibilities of paternity are spread among all the possible biological fathers or placed on the shoulders of one or more of the mother's male kinsfolk;
2. in countries with high divorce rates it is possible for a child to have a succession of sociological fathers: its legitimacy depends primarily on whether it had one such father when it was new-born;
3. in many societies a child, once born, can be made legitimate by adoption, and it is not invariably necessary that the adopter be male.

KINSHIP, BLOOD, DESCENT

Family depends on kinship, which Malinowski defined as follows:

> The personal bonds based on procreation, socially interpreted; together with the wider bonds derived from the primary ones by the process of gradual extensions which occur in all communities during the life-history of the individual.[4]

Among savages, he says, the extensions are both more numerous and more rigidly systematized than with us; furthermore, they are more frequently backed up by fictions of totemic descent, by ideas about one-sided procreation or by theories that assert a mystical identity between kinsfolk. Biological kinship between members of one species is something we share with other animals, but kinship as described above is peculiar to mankind. Kinship in man is modified by human perception of it and by social interpretation. After language, it is far and away the most important human institution there is. It controls law, family life, economics, social organization and social hierarchies, reproduction and child rearing. It strongly influences morality, religion, art and politics. Malinowski mentions many examples of the control and influence of kinship on other human institutions, and it is not difficult to add to his list. Individual human beings are named after kinsfolk. An orphan's first substitute parent, in virtually every human society, is a kinswoman, usually an aunt or a grandmother. Kingship is the right to govern, and in most countries it is based on descent. (Poland was an exception when it had kings.) Property and inheritance depend largely on kinship links. In most societies the work a man does is a matter determined by family tradition. The Japanese are said to worship their ancestors, and Europeans give to popes, priests, monks and nuns the titles of 'Father', 'Brother', 'Mother', 'Sister'. We call our countries of origin the Motherland or the Fatherland. Even the planet is called Mother Earth.

One of the most important aspects of the notion of kinship is the idea of shared blood. This gives rise to ideas like that of 'blue' blood, which is aristocratic, and that of impure blood (or mixed blood), which is the blood of people whose parents were of different races or different classes, or were simply bad, or criminal, or not married to each other. The saying 'It's in his blood' means 'He has inherited this trait (or whatever) from his ancestors, along with his blood.' The idea that blood, through being mixed racially or socially, becomes bad or impure in some way seems quite common. The mixed, bad and impure blood goes with criminality and immorality: this commonplace thought is well-expressed by Kipling, when he describes some low-class woman as 'a Negroid-Jewess-Cuban; with morals to match'.[5] Similarly, the word 'mongrel', when it is applied insultingly to human beings (something which, according to the *Oxford English Dictionary*, has been happening since 1542), means 'a person not of pure race: the offspring of parents of different nationalities or of high and low birth'. The despised half-caste and the despised bastard were no doubt often one and the same person, since restrictions on marriage are often racial. Defenders of 'racial purity' frequently compare the different races of men with different species of animals. Lower races are compared with apes, and half-castes are called 'misbegotten': bastards too are regularly denied humanity or are spoken of as half-human.[6]

The idea of shared blood relates to the notion of descent, which is an even more important aspect of the notion of kinship. Now, there is more than one way in which descent can be traced, and this is associated with the fact that there is more than one set of rules whereby a (living) family can be delineated. These different ways of tracing descent and different sets of rules for including and excluding people in and from families are among the many factors which, it seems reasonable to suppose, determine the degree of severity with which illicit birth and illegitimate children are treated.

It is characteristic of human beings to fear death and to hope for personal immortality. Possibly this is a human version of the universal instinct for self-preservation. One way in which a man can strive for immortality is to create living, physical replicas of himself – sons. When the family is delineated by the male name and/or the male blood line the ideological significance of the kinship link between father and son reinforces, and is reinforced by, this desire for immortality; the whole thing can acquire religious importance. A man's desire for sons is deeply respected, like his desire for Heaven – indeed, it is an analogue for that desire, as can be seen from Scripture, wherein Jehovah is reported as repeatedly promising various favoured individuals that their seed shall be as the sand on the shore and shall live forever. Obviously, the desire for living, physical replicas can be thwarted in two ways: by the birth of females (hence the birth of a daughter is a symbol, in the Koran, for a valueless gift)[7] and by uncertainty about the paternity of sons. This must surely be one of the main reasons why adultery has been punished by death and why bastards and superfluous female children have been destroyed at birth. If a child is thought of as an economic liability (as is the case in most of modern Europe) rather than as an economic asset (as is the case in much of Africa), there are secular as well as mystical reasons for hostility towards the illegitimate. Finally, a child is an obvious symbol of potency; thus in France a man who wittingly or unwittingly accepts his wife's lover's child into his family and lineage is a famous figure of fun, the farcical cuckold, who is generally represented on stage as sexually incompetent if not completely impotent.

Our secular and mystical ideas about descent, about our ancestors and our descendants, are deeply influenced by the ways in which descent is traced. The concepts of ancestor and descendant are modified by social interpretation. For example, if an Englishman asks a genealogist to help him to trace his forbears, he will want primarily to find out about the line of males which ends with his father – taking it backwards in time, he will want to know about his father, his father's father, his father's father's father and so on. He may or may not also wish, 'as a matter of interest', to trace his forbears 'on the mother's side', which means the line of males which ends with his mother's father – taking it backwards in time, the line which runs from his mother's father via his mother's father's father to more and more distant fathers and grandfathers. A typical Englishman is unlikely to want to know much about the line or 'rope' which goes back via his mother's father's mother's father's mother, for instance.[8] Indeed, individuals traced through this line or rope he will not really think of as belonging to his family, or as proper ancestors at all, unless one of them happens to have done some deed or held some office of real importance in the history of his country. Tracing the lineage of both males and females through males is for us so easy and natural that it is like breathing air; we hardly notice that we do it and normally never consider the possibility that there may be other principles for delineating a family in time. If we do come across other methods, they may strike us as extraordinarily intricate, and even as somehow artificial. The books written by white anthropologists about African methods of tracing descent are extremely learned works, and some of their pages look like diagrams of the insides of computers. There are systems of tracing lineage which are so strange to the European mind, it is said, that the European mind cannot comprehend them. The Navajo system is apparently a notorious example of such a system.[9]

Patrilineal descent systems trace descent for both males and females through males. Matrilineal systems trace descent for both males and females through females. Both these systems are called unilineal. Some people have systems of double descent, which can take one of two forms: either they trace males through the male (or female) line and females through the female (or male) line – i.e., they trace the descent of male individuals in one way and the descent of female individuals in another way; or they trace the descent of all individuals, both male and female, in a way which involves reference to both 'sides', the male and female, with the details being modified, perhaps, by considerations having to do with property, jobs, residence, etc.[10]

In matrilineal societies it is possible to ignore or minimize the biological role of the begetter. Malinowski reported[11] that the Trobriand Islanders seemed not to realize that sexual intercourse is liable to produce babies. Some people think that the Trobrianders were pulling Dr Malinowski's leg. Others think that Dr Malinowski had a deep-seated Freudian wish to believe that these happy children of Nature were, like ideal European children, ignorant of the facts of life. But surely the most probable explanation is that the Trobrianders must have known that sexual intercourse is neither *necessary* for the production of babies (since semen can be introduced into a woman by means other than actual intercourse) nor *sufficient* for the production of babies (since some couples are infertile, for natural or artificial reasons). The Trobrianders' perception of this obvious truth, their relaxed and free-and-easy sexual customs and their matrilineal system of tracing lineage combined into an ideology which attributed a minimal significance to the paternal role in procreation.

In a patrilineal society, on the other hand, a family is essentially delineated by the blood line which goes from father to son. The role of the father is therefore emphasized. Of course, even in the most male-dominated communities the mother's role cannot be completely ignored – there is no way to pretend that she has *nothing* to do with childbirth. But her role can be seen as, and treated as, accidental, inessential. A. I. Richards remarks[12] that in societies with patrilineal systems of tracing descent the ideology of decent can give to the begetter a symbolic child-bearing role, so that the father is regarded as having placed the infant in a receptacle (the mother), where it remains until he and it are ready for its introduction into his family and lineage. (There are traces of this fantasy in the writings of Freud.)

When male blood is what delineates a family every married couple wants a son, for without sons the family itself will die out. Anyone who has ever been in a maternity ward in England will know that mothers who have had baby girls are to some extent commiserated with, especially if they belong to immigrant communities with patriarchal traditions. Nursing staff and doctors are liable to congratulate women who have had sons on being 'lucky' or 'clever'. Natural parents want sons, but adopting parents in England show a preference for girls; this is just the other side of the same ideological coin. A boy who does not share his parents' blood is a sort of cuckoo-child; he is entitled to the family name and can pass it on to a line of males biologically unrelated to his adopters. An adopted girl, on the other hand, if she is a reasonably successful female, will bear the surname of the adopters only until such time as she marries and joins another family, one delineated by the surname of her husband. Girls do not make up an essential part of a (European) family line, so it does not matter much if an adopted girl does not share any of her adopted parents' blood.

The European concept of a family closely links names, property rights, jobs and power. Names, jobs, property and power are passed from male to male. When property and power are substantial we (Europeans) speak of dynasties and of dynastic power and dynastic succession.

The link between names and power and property is interestingly illustrated by the last will and testament of Mayer Rothschild, the first notable member of that remarkable family. Rothschild made his will in 1812, shortly before his death. To prevent the 'dilution of the family' by sons-in-law, Mayer Rothschild willed as follows:

> My daughter, sons-in-law, and their heirs, shall have no part whatsoever in the firm of M. A. Rothschild and Sons . . . nor the right to examine the said business, its books, inventories, papers, etc. . . . I shall never forgive my children if they against my parental wishes take it upon themselves to disturb my sons in the peaceful possession of their business.[13]

During the next hundred years many Rothschild women married Rothschild cousins bearing the Rothschild name.

An illegitimate person is a kind of outsider. What he is outside is the (normal) family. He has biological kin, of course, but, from the social point of view, he has no kin except for his mother – and even his mother might give him up and disappear. The lack of a legal tie with the male parent is, in European societies, marked by the social and legal fact that an illegitimate individual has no proper surname. To have a name is to be someone; to lack a name is to be a kind of no one, and namelessness is part of the traditional stigma of bastardy. The importance of naming has been recognized by certain countries (e.g., Finland) in legislation designed to remove the stigma: recent laws make it possible to give a child, whether born in wedlock or not, either its mother's or its father's surname, thus ensuring that every child has a legally recognized surname.

To be born into a community which traces descent matrilineally would seem to entail automatic membership of a lineage. In fact, it is not the case that no stigma is attached to illegitimacy in matrilineal societies; neither is it the case that the legitimacy/illegitimacy distinction cannot exist in such societies. Other factors also seem to affect the matter, as can be illustrated by examples.

In some parts of Jamaica people born out of wedlock outnumber those born in it, and these many technically illegitimate individuals are not, as a general rule, legitimated subsequently. In such communities no really serious stigma can attach to the status of illegitimacy. All the same, the rulers of Jamaica have at different times spoken of the high illegitimacy rate as a serious social problem. But it may be worth asking whether Jamaican illegitimacy really is illegitimacy.

What exactly counts as illegitimacy in a particular country must depend on the laws of that country and also on its customs. In Jamaica the law is based on English law, but the customs are modifications of customs originally imported from three different continents – Europe, India and Africa. Since the English were the original ruling caste, it was their marriage and property institutions which became the law of the country, and when it is said that large numbers of Jamaicans are illegitimate, what is meant is that they are illegitimate in terms of that law.

English law was, of course, well understood by Englishmen. The marriage customs of immigrants from India were, in their turn, sufficiently similar to those of the English to mesh reasonably with English law. For historical reasons too, the English ruling class did not find Indian customs completely foreign or strange. Also, the Indians in the West Indies did not go there as slaves but as indentured labourers or as free immigrants. Their customs have, no doubt, been altered by transplantation but not perverted by slavery. The case must have been very different with the Africans. Traditional African law is said not to be perspicuous to European minds, and anyway slave owners do not generally take any trouble to find out about the customs and laws of enslaved peoples. To this day it is not known for certain whether the social organization of Jamaicans of African descent derives mainly from African traditions or is, rather, the product of slavery.

In Jamaica before Independence there was a tendency to regard the mating habits of the white community, and those of the Indian community too, as normal but to think of the habits of the Negroes and mulattos as aberrant.[14]

Indians in Jamaica characteristically marry young, especially the girls. Marriages are still sometimes arranged by parents. Over 75 per cent of Indians living in Jamaica marry only once. The wife, on marrying, leaves her father's home and joins her husband's household, and the children of the marriage live with their father and mother, bear their father's name and are supported mainly by him. Shiva Naipaul's novel *Fireflies* describes just such a marriage and just such a household.[15] Not all Hindu and Muslim weddings are formally registered at a Registry Office, so that the offspring of some Indian marriages are technically illegitimate, unbeknown to the parents. But it is not this kind of illegitimacy that is thought to constitute a problem.

Jamaicans of African descent who belong to the working class characteristically enter into several successive conjugal unions, each of which may last for some time but only one of which, the last, is likely to be a legally recognized marriage. Indian girls marry almost as soon as they reach child-bearing age, whereas women of African descent marry when they have passed the age of child bearing and after they have in fact borne children, quite possibly to several different men. Some African unions involve a shared household; others are visiting arrangements.

In 1956 more than half the children living in Negro families in Grenville (Grenada), Kingston (Jamaica) and rural Jamaica as a whole were in households run by the mother, or by the grandmother (usually the maternal), or by relatives other than the father. In Kingston only 34 per cent of children in such communities lived in the same household as their fathers.[16] Support for such children looks exceedingly haphazard, for it is shared between the mother, the maternal grandmother and the absent father in a number of ad hoc ways. In a typical family group the father will send contributions of money to the mother either when he feels like it or at regular intervals. The children may move around between different households, and this interferes with their schooling, of course, since schooling arrangements are based on the assumption that each child has one home. Negroes who move up into the middle class tend to adopt the mating customs of the white man. They get married formally, set up households and send their children to school every day. For people of this class illegitimacy can be a stigma, though (it is said) not a serious one.[17]

Some anthropologists believe that the family arrangements of Negroes and mulattoes in the West Indies derive from the matrilineal and matrifocal family structures traditional in parts of West Africa. If the theory is correct, then the kin groups made up of mother, grandmother and children, which are visited by fathers but not centred on them, are not abberrant forms created by Jamaican promiscuity but the lineal descendants of West African matrifocal kin groups. This theory was put forward by the anthropologist M. Herskovits,[18] and it is given some support by facts known about Jamaican Negro ideas concerning land tenure. When Jamaicans of African descent were given the chance to own land they adopted a system of tenure which is at variance with the English system of primogeniture enshrined in the law of Jamaica. They themselves say that the system comes to them from grandparents and great-grandparents. According to the Jamaican Negro system, land does not belong to individuals but to families; it cannot be sold but is supposed to pass from one generation of a family to the next. There are two possible rules of transfer: transfer by the blood, in which family land passes from mother to daughters and sons, and transfer by the name (probably the slave owner's name), in which the land passes from father to son. These rules of transfer were adopted, apparently spontaneously, at the time of the abolition of slavery, and were still being operated in parts of Jamaica when the island became independent.

A white man giving a piece of land to one of his freed slaves thought of himself as giving it to an individual, but the slave took it, as it were, on behalf of a family, on behalf of himself and all his descendants, matrilineally or patrilineally determined as the case may be. Anyone in the direct line of descent as thus determined was considered to have an unquestionable right to live on the family land. In times of economic slump, therefore, plots of family land became rather crowded. Family land was the inheritance of the Negro child, whether he was technically legitimate or not. It represented his security and, in a way, his legitimacy, for his right depended on descent.[19]

In opposition to Herskovits's theory, it has been argued that the mating customs and child-rearing habits of Jamaican Negroes resemble those found wherever there is slavery or a history of slavery, serfdom or very extreme poverty. In such situations neither parent can offer any security to the child, and therefore the breakdown occurs of whatever system was in operation before slavery or serfdom intervened. The child stays with the mother purely and simply because of their close biological tie, and both live in penury. This kind of 'matrifocal family', it is argued, has nothing to do with matrifocal family *systems*.

But surely Herskovits's theory and the slavery theory are not incompatible? Present customs may well be the result of many factors; they may well be the result of the superimposition of slavery upon traditional systems of West African law, followed by modifications due to Christian ideas, and then by further modifications due to the individual efforts of Jamaican Negroes to rise in the social scale.

According to most of the traditional non-Islamic systems of African law,[20] a proper marriage required the transfer of property between the kinsfolk of the two marriage partners.

Generally, this was a transfer of cattle from the man's kinsfolk to the woman's kinsfolk. Marriages were arranged, at least in the sense that the two sets of kinsfolk were supposed to initiate and organize the property transfer, and a sexual union without such a transfer was not proper legal marriage. If the transfer was unsatisfactory or incomplete, the bride might well return to her family, rather as a woman whose marriage has been declared null in a traditional European society returns to her family. It is obvious that slavery must have rendered traditional African marriage totally impossible, since slaves do not own property. Anti-slavery organizations claimed that slavery as an institution bred sexual immorality, alleging that healthy male slaves were treated as stallions and encouraged to beget as many new slaves as possible, whilst female slaves were regarded either as brood mares to these stallions or as the slave owners' concubines. So it seems that Christian marriages did not automatically replace African ones in the slave societies of the West Indies.

Traditionally in Africa everyone was supposed to marry, and virtually everyone did marry: hence, by and large, irregularly conceived children would be those born of adultery. Adultery was everywhere a punishable offence (in some tribes the punishment was death), but since children were highly valued, the child born of adultery would still belong to a lineage – his mother's in a matrilineal community, his mother's husband's in a patrilineal one.

Thus if a people has a patrilineal descent system, that does not necessarily mean that those of its children who are born irregularly will lack a name and lineage. Conversely, a child born of adultery into a matrilineal society is not automatically entitled to a name and lineage – he might not even be allowed to live. For example, the Nayar of Kerala, India, a matrilineal and polyandrous people,[21] had a notion of illegitimacy which related to the idea of caste and which meant that a child conceived irregularly could not belong to a lineage. The customs of the Nayar have been described by the anthropologist E. K. Gough.[22] She relates how before the British came to India the Nayar (at that time still polyandrous) lived in villages in sibling groups under the guardianship of the oldest male. Each girl had several recognized sexual partners, sometimes as many as 12, usually about three or four. These men did not live with her; they lived with their brothers and sisters, and she lived with her brothers and sisters. Each of the visiting husbands was supposed to give the wife gifts and to make payments to a midwife when she was confined. Two or three men or more would acknowledge possible biological paternity each time a child was born. If all the husbands refused to acknowledge paternity, it was assumed that the girl must have taken as a lover some man of a lower caste.

> she must then either be expelled by her lineage or killed by her matrilineal kinsmen. I am uncertain as to the precise fate of the child in such a case, but there is no doubt at all that he could not be accepted as a member of his lineage and caste. I do not know whether he was killed, or became a slave: almost certainly he must have shared the fate of his mother.[23]

Gough reports that even in modern times (1949) it was still absolutely necessary that one man or several men agreed to pay the confinement fees when a girl had a baby; if no man would do so, the girl suffered total ostracism and was driven from the village by her own kinsmen on the orders of the village assembly, which would impose ostracism on the kinsfolk themselves if they disobeyed. Normally, however, one or more of the husbands would agree to pay the expenses of the confinement. The upkeep of the child thereafter was the responsibility of the mother's kinsmen. Every Nayar girl had a ritual husband to whom she was ceremoniously married before puberty, and any girl who was not married before the onset of puberty would be put to death; sometimes, therefore, the kinsmen would hide the fact of puberty until a ritual husband could be found.

Legitimacy and illegitimacy are often connected with matters having to do with caste, race and religion. As one might expect, this is particularly true in the subcontinent of India. In Nayar marriage the ritual husband stood as representative of his caste group and symbolized the correctness of the paternity of the woman's future children. The duties of the visiting husbands were to provide the woman with children and to acknowledge biological paternity; such acknowledgement reaffirmed the caste correctness (i.e. *the legitimacy in Nayar terms*) of the children. The proper method of acknowledgement was to pay the midwife; payment, formally legitimized the child, as it were.

It would seem from these examples, then, that the concepts of legitimacy and illegitimacy do not depend solely on the existence of a patriarchal patrilineal social system.

CHAPTER 8

The Disabilities of Illegitimacy

The traditional disabilities of illegitimacy are legal and customary. They have material and social consequences which vary from time to time and place to place.

LINEAGE

In Christendom the general rule was that a male bastard could found a lineage (i.e., pass on a name) but could not belong to one that already existed. Strictly speaking, a bastard had no relatives in law and no surname. However, it was and still is customary for illegitimate children of either sex in patrilineal societies to be known by the surname of the maternal grandfather. In fact, in parts of East Africa an illegitimate child is called a 'grandfather's child' because of this. In Europe an adult male bastard may take his own father's Christian name as a surname, or he may take his wife's father's surname, or he may take or be given a nickname, which then becomes his surname. Such surnames can then be passed onto the man's own legitimate children under the common law. The old rule that a bastard could found a lineage but not belong to one already in existence was expressed in various ways: for example, in Scotland until 1836 a bastard with no legitimate descendants was debarred in law from making a will.[1]

INHERITANCE

Most European countries have or have had laws which restrict testamentary freedom. The main point of such laws has always been to prevent men from disinheriting their dependants and leaving them as a charge on the community, but sometimes the laws governing inheritance have been used to bring about other social goods – for instance, the preservation of farmland or the prevention of the sale of vital land or industry to foreigners. Whether or not a man makes a will, the state or the Church, or both, will take a certain percentage of his estate when he dies. When a man dies intestate the usual rule is that his property goes to his wife and children after it has been taxed. If he has no wife or children, his property will go to other kin, if he has any.

Under the Napoleonic Code a Frenchman had to will at least two-thirds of his estate to his legitimate direct descendants, and the oldest son had special rights. Unmarried people, on the other hand, were free to leave property to whomsoever they pleased. In Russia under Stalin testamentary freedom was very restricted. A man had to will his property to his legitimate children, if he had any, though he did not have to leave them equal shares. A man with no legitimate children had to leave his property to other kinsfolk. A man with no living kin could leave his property either to the state, or to the Russian Communist Party, or to certain scientific and cultural organizations, or, finally, to an illegitimate child.

Generally speaking, until the twentieth century illegitimate children did not count as kin, so that a child born out of wedlock could not inherit if its father died intestate. In some systems obstacles were placed in the way of willing property to illegitimate children. On the other hand, in some places illegitimate people have had rights of inheritance against their mother or even against their maternal grandparents. Wherever the possibility of inheriting from a natural father exists in a legal system it is hedged about with rules designed partly to protect the rights of legitimate children and partly to lay down the kinds and degrees of proof needed to establish biological paternity.

THE LYING-IN

Nowadays some legitimate children are born at home, and others are born in hospitals or maternity homes. Until the twentieth century, however, an illegitimate child (unless it was the offspring of a rich man's acknowledged mistress, for instance) would be more likely to be born in a workhouse or 'ditch-deliver'd by a drab'. Fathers were expected to expel unmarried pregnant daughters from the family home, and what they were expected to do they normally did, even as recently as the 1940s. Respectable people would not employ, or continue to employ, a servant girl who became pregnant. It seems that hospitals were allowed to turn unmarried pregnant women away from their doors, at least in the eighteenth century. In 1788 the philanthropist John Howard wrote *An Account of the Principal Lazarettes of Europe*,[2] in which he included descriptions of some maternity hospitals: it is obvious from the titles of, and the advertisements for, these hospitals that they were intended only for properly married women.[3] In the twentieth century public hospitals do not turn unmarried pregnant women away, but until about 1960 or so doctors and nursing staff were in general rude and unpleasant to such patients. Some doctors refused anaesthetics to unmarried women in childbirth 'to teach them a lesson'.[4]

INFANT MORTALITY

In countries which keep records of births and deaths it is known that there is a persistent and significant difference between the infant mortality rates of legitimate and illegitimate children. Roughly speaking, the difference ranges from 50 to 150 per cent. English and Norwegian data on infant mortality for four sample years of this century confirm the discrepancy:

Country	Year	Infant morality per 1000 live births	
		Legitimate	Illegitimate
England	1914	100	207
England	1918	91	186
Norway	1955	19.7	44.3
England	1973	16	23

Source: NCOPF.

Many reasons have been suggested in attempts to explain this continuing difference. It is said that illegitimate babies are less likely to be breast-fed than legitimate babies, either because the unmarried mother has to leave her child with other people while she goes out to work, or because the child is given up for adoption or placed in an institution. It is said that the health of unmarried mothers is less good than the health of married mothers because they have less money and because they find it difficult to take advantage of the prenatal care made available to pregnant women in public hospitals. In England, for example, patients attending prenatal clinics in public hospitals sometimes have to wait for hours before seeing a doctor or midwife. This is an inconvenient arrangement even for patients whose time is completely free and an impossible one for women who work – especially those who are not supposed to be pregnant in the first place. It is also argued that unmarried mothers are, on average, younger than married mothers, and for very young women childbirth is more dangerous than for women over 18. It seems probable that all these matters play some part in raising the infant mortality rate of illegitimate children above the rate for other children.

INFANTICIDE

One of the worst disadvantages suffered by the illegitimate child is his proneness, when in infancy or in embryo, to become the object of deliberate acts of destruction.

In the Middle Ages the peasant's labour was the lord's source of wealth, and it seems unlikely that this gentleman would bother his head too much about the legitimacy or otherwise of his serfs. On the other hand, canon law laid down punishments for fornication, and for giving birth to bastards, and for hiding the births of such children. As we have seen, laws 'for ye discouragement of bastardy' remained in force until comparatively recent times. When infant death rates were in any case very high the temptation secretly to destroy a bastard baby must have been very strong; there was no other or easier way, probably, to avoid the punishments, stigma and shame. Punishment, stigma, ostracism and destitution were the 'fate worse than death'. Folklore and fiction both reinforce the reasonable supposition that over the centuries very large numbers of illegitimate babies have been done to death by their mothers, by other relatives or by midwives. Such deeds still occur from time to time, even in modern industrial societies with permissive attitudes towards sexuality and illegitimacy. (A few years ago, for instance, *The Times* carried a report of the trial in the USA of a young nun accused of murdering a baby to which she had given birth in secret.)

In several modern societies it is regarded as perfectly natural that most illegitimate conceptions should end in abortion and a good thing that most, in fact, do. The prevention of illegitimate birth is one of the main premises (stated or unstated) of arguments supporting the legalisation of abortion on demand.

MAINTENANCE AND SUPPORT

Under the *filius nullius* rule no one had a legal obligation to support an illegitimate child. But *no one* did not necessarily mean *no one*: it meant, rather, *no legal person* – in effect, *no man*.

For the mother of an illegitimate child did have a customary obligation (which eventually became a legal obligation) to care for the child, at least until such time as she could hand it over to someone else, or until she had it taken away from her.

In the sixteenth century laws were made in England which enabled a mother or a parish to sue the putative father of an illegitimate child for a contribution towards its maintenance. Other countries had similar arrangements. Although such laws were difficult to enforce, it was surely a bad idea to abolish them, as France did in 1803, or to curtail the mother's right to sue, as England did in 1834. In certain other countries legislation became more humane rather than less so. Thus although Norwegian law did not explicitly recognize paternal responsibility for the maintenance of illegitimate children until 1722, a law of that year and subsequent legislation of 1821, 1892 and 1915 were designed to help preserve the child by helping the mother care for it.[5] The playwright Henrik Ibsen was ordered in 1846 to help support an illegitimate boy thought to be his son: he had to keep up the payments for 18 years!

The illegitimate infant's total or partial dependence on its mother, the economically weaker parent, has always been the source of its most serious material disabilities, including infanticide and abortion. When women were economically dependent, property-less and confined by custom (or even by law) to types of work for which they received low wages or payment in kind, it was completely inevitable that illegitimate babies should be left on doorsteps, in baby farms and in foundling homes, and completely inevitable too that the infant mortality rate of illegitimate babies should be much higher than that of legitimate children.

Nowadays, of course, women are able to earn money in a variety of jobs and are allowed to own property (though generally speaking they are not widely represented in the class of millionaires): all the same, the unmarried mother can still expect to be treated as a special case. For instance, in the course of a controversy which appeared in the columns of the *New Statesman and Nation* in 1939, an anonymous correspondent wrote:

> If I was to sign this letter people would first, in the name of virtue, deprive me of my livelihood, thereby making it impossible for me to support my child and myself; and then they would complain that I had (by their own action) become a charge on the community.

More recently, in December 1972, a document was drawn up setting out recommendations for the granting of maternity leave for women teachers by the local education authorities (LEAs). It outlined the agreed period of maternity leave, the rates of pay and other benefits, then stated:

> These provisions do not apply to unmarried women teachers except insofar as the Local Education Authority may at its discretion choose to apply them according to the circumstances of each case.[6]

The organizations represented at the conference which drew up the document making the recommendations included the Association of Education Committees, the Association of Municipal Corporations, the County Councils' Association, the National Union of Teachers and the National Association of Headmasters. It may seem surprising that the teachers' own unions agreed to exclude some of their members from the benefits enjoyed by others. But a survey conducted by the National Council for the Unmarried Mother and her Child in the 1970s showed that headmasters and other teachers disliked having an unmarried mother teaching in the same school as themselves. Some headmasters asked their LEAs either to sack a teacher who was an unmarried mother or to transfer her to another school. Others exerted pressure on the woman herself, suggesting she resign or apply for transfer. Some such women were told they could only stay on in their jobs if they wore wedding rings and pretended to be married. Others had to agree to live in a different borough from the school and to keep away from the parents of the children at the school. In these matters headmasters and members of the National Union of Teachers were usually backed up by their LEAs. The discretion of the LEAs themselves was exercised by asking the unmarried teacher to resign, for example, or by refusing maternity leave (thus enforcing resignation), or by issuing notices of 'temporary dismissal'. It is difficult to see how these activities of headmasters and LEAs could be of any discernible benefit to a school: the main immediate effect must surely have been disruptive. Perhaps the heads and the LEAs decided that 'ye discouragement of bastardy' was justifiable from the point of view of long-term overall utility.

SEPARATION FROM KIN

Institutions

In England, Europe, North America and Australasia it is normal for illegitimate infants to be separated, temporarily or permanently, from their biological kin.

In the early part of the nineteenth century certain charitable organizations set out to save fallen women (i.e., unmarried pregnant girls or unmarried mothers) from starvation or prostitution. The workhouses were normally the first ports of call for such people, but although a baby could be taken in permanently, its mother, if able-bodied, was expected to leave and find work. In any case, the workhouse was exceedingly unpopular as a refuge. Going into the workhouse involved considerable hardship. No personal belongings could be taken in, and for a long time inmates had to wear uniform. The reforms of 1834 were not aimed at making the arrangement less harsh. The sexes were segregated, and this included the separation of parents and children. (For example, Charles Chaplin, a legitimate child who entered the Lambeth workhouse with his mother and older brother in 1895, was separated from his mother – he was 6 years old.)[7] There were no arrangements inside the workhouse for visits between parents and children or between brothers and sisters. If a child was inside the workhouse and its parents outside, a monthly visit was permitted: it seems probable that this rule may have applied only to legitimate children, the Guardians exercising their discretion in the case of illegitimate children. Children living inside the workhouse were not permitted to visit parents outside. The main qualification needed for post of Master of the Workhouse was physical strength, since the job involved dealing with any adult male inmates who might become violent. The clergy sometimes complained that the masters of the local workhouses refused to allow them to visit their parishoners inside. The stated policy of making the workhouses as unpleasant as possible conflicted not only with the duties of the clergy but also with those of the doctor, the nurse and, later, the school teacher; it also, obviously, conflicted with the rights of parents.

These, then, were some of the reasons why an unmarried pregnant girl or unmarried mother might need or wish to seek refuge in some place other than a workhouse. No doubt, many girls and women who were ineligible for the workhouse or unwilling to enter it became prostitutes, this being the fate of large numbers of working-class females in the eighteenth and nineteenth centuries anyway.

The first home specifically for unmarried mothers in England was opened in London in 1805. It was called the Dalston Refuge. Later came the London Female Penitentiary in 1807, the School of Discipline for Destitute Girls in 1825, the Oxford Female Penitentiary in 1839 and the British Penitent

Female Refuge in 1840.[8] Various authorities, such as the magistrates or, in the University cities, the Proctors, had the power to incarcerate girls in some of these 'homes'; others were true refuges, in that entry was voluntary. Such refuges were also found in Europe, including European Russia, where they were commonly known as 'Magdalen homes'. Tolstoy comments on the fact that women of his own class sometimes occupied themselves with charities designed for the rescue of 'Magdalens', many of whom would have been seduced and abandoned by men of that same aristocratic class.[9]

In the nineteenth century the general rule was to separate the mother from the child. The idea was that the child – if it survived – would be brought up in an institution of some kind, run either by the Guardians of the Poor or by a private charity, so that it could not come under the bad influence of its immoral female parent. Meanwhile the mother would be disciplined and, if possible, reformed.

Mothers who wished to maintain contact with their babies might do so by keeping away from the workhouses, homes and refuges and instead taking the baby to a baby farmer. These private individuals would look after the child while the mother worked. In England baby farmers were not subject to registration and overseeing until 1872. Dreadful scandals occurred. In 1870, for instance, a baby farmer called Margaret Walters was tried for the murder of 16 infants who had been left in her care; she was found guilty and hanged. She was not the only one: in that same year 276 dead bodies of infants were found in London. Such horrors were not new, but they struck at the Victorian conscience. New laws were passed, the Infant Life Protection Acts of 1872[10] and 1897.[11] The Registration of Births Act of 1874 made it easier to detect murder by previously anonymous midwives and baby farmers.[12] In 1908 the so-called 'Children's Charter' more or less abolished baby farming in its old form by setting up regulations for the fostering of children with which the baby farmers apparently found it difficult to comply.[13]

In 1909 an Italian, a former Consul-General in London, wrote a letter to *The Times*. It read as follows:

> More money is wasted in England prosecuting unfortunate

> mothers than would suffice to make good citizens of the number of children (sometimes born, sometimes unborn) who are made away with solely for the reason that in this country no provision is made for them. Further . . . the children so born are not the scum of the population but largely the children of domestic servants, factory hands, shop assistants, and the better class of village girls, all of whom, if given an opportunity, can earn a living and keep their little ones.[14]

When the Boards of Guardians were asked in 1910 to make recommendations on the matter of bastardy, however, they were less concerned with the fate of illegitimate children and unmarried mothers than with the rights of the rate payers. The Royal Commission on the Poor Laws[15] received 169 recommendations from the Boards about bastardy, the great majority of which suggested more or stricter punishments and deterrents for unmarried mothers. Many Boards asked for greater powers to enable them to detain unmarried mothers in the workhouse, so that their unpaid domestic work therein could be set against the cost to the rate payer of supporting illegitimate children.[16]

The first British hostel for unmarried mothers which allowed such a mother to take her infant in with her was opened in 1871.[17] It was set up by a women's organization called the Female Mission to the Fallen, and the theory of the females of the Mission was that if mothers were allowed to care for their babies themselves in the ordinary way, they would develop ties of affection and a sense of responsibility which, for one thing, might prevent them from harming or neglecting the child and, for another, might have an improving and stabilizing influence on their own moral character. Not an altogether idiotic theory, though no doubt the ladies who thought of it were well jeered at the time.

To provide a temporary refuge for a mother and baby was one thing; to provide a permanent home and means of support was quite another. There were no social security payments and no Claimants' Unions in those days. Still, an attempt was made to deal with this mammoth problem by a London charity which, in 1912, set up a refuge called the Day Servants' Hostel.[18] This hostel allowed a mother to keep her baby, supporting it by working as a daily (i.e., not a 'live-in') domestic servant. The hostel must have been reasonably successful in its aims because many similar ones were opened in the following decades, and in the 1950s there were mother-and-baby homes of this kind in most parts of Britain. In 1974 the NCOPF issued a directory of accommodation available for unmarried mothers,[19] which listed 75 different flatlet and bedsittingroom schemes in England and Wales. Since then the number has diminished, for a variety of reasons. First, the practice of expelling an unmarried pregnant daughter from her father's house has become far less common than it once was. Among the indigenous population it is probably highly unusual nowadays: some immigrant groups, however – for example, those from the Indian subcontinent – still practise such expulsion. Second, there has been a continuing increase in the availability and size of social security payments. Third, the number of women in paid employment has increased, which seems to indicate that more jobs are available to women. Fourth, English law now permits abortion.

All the same, in spite of the attempts made by charities and, later, by social services departments to preserve, at least in many cases, the links between mother and child, the most usual solutions to the problems of maintaining illegitimate children were and still are full or part-time institutionalization of the child, adoption and fostering. Even today about half the children in institutional care in the countries of the European Economic Community are illegitimate.

During the second half of the nineteenth century a gradual separation took place between the various functions of the workhouse. Destitute children, insane adults, the aged poor, etc. were at last seen to have somewhat different needs. 'Separate schools' were built for the children: these were boarding schools attached to workhouses. In 1862 the Certified Schools Act[20] empowered the Guardians to place children in certain hostels called 'schools' and run by private charities. Such 'schools' could be certified after satisfying inspectors from the Boards of Guardians that the children were adequately fed and clothed. The day-to-day running of these establishments was left to the people in direct charge and to the charities concerned. Official policy favoured the certified schools, which were run more cheaply than workhouse schools. The people entrusted with the care of the children were usually untrained, ill-educated and not particularly well-equipped to teach the children or to care for them when they were sick. Discipline was very severe. At first teachers, often trades teachers, were employed in the workhouse schools and certified schools; later, after the Education Act of 1870,[21] the children could be sent each day to the local elementary school. Until 1944 no public money was ever wasted on the secondary education of such children. They were expected, on leaving school, to go into domestic service if they were girls and into labouring jobs or the army if they were boys.

The best-known of the private charities in England that were concerned with the care of homeless children is probably Dr Barnardo's. Thomas Barnardo was born in Dublin in 1845 and came to London in 1866 to train as a medical missionary. His intention at that time was to spend his life as a missionary in China. In 1866–7 there was a cholera epidemic in East London, and Barnardo volunteered to work there. The sight of the large numbers of homeless children in East London persuaded him to stay in England. While still a student, he opened his East End Juvenile Mission in 1867. In 1870 he opened a boy's home in Stepney and in 1876 the Girls' Village Home in Barkingside in Essex. This latter was a very large establishment: in 1930 there were 1400 children living in it. In 1882 Barnardo organized the emigration to Canada of a party of destitute boys, then, in 1883, that of a similar party of girls. In 1886 he opened a home in Kent which he called the Babies' Castle. He founded a total of 90 homes, rescued and trained 59,348 destitute children and assisted another 250,000. In 40 years he raised from private donors a total of over £3.5 million sterling. Barnardo resisted the idea, prevalent in his time, that illegitimate children are hereditarily defective. He argued that the ill-health common among illegitimate children was caused by environmental factors such as malnutrition.

Barnardo's father's ancestors left Spain in the eighteenth century to escape religious persecution: his mother was a Quaker. Barnardo himself was fiercely anti-Catholic, and only Protestant teachings were provided in Barnardo homes. This led inevitably to rows with the Roman Catholic Church and with Roman Catholic parents.[22] During 1889–91 he was involved in much litigation. In 1891 it was agreed that Roman

Catholic and Jewish children must be released from Barnardo homes if there were places available for them in Roman Catholic and Jewish homes respectively. Possibly the legal battles spurred the Roman Catholics and Jews to build more orphanages of their own.

Barnardo died in 1905 and was given a public funeral. He is buried in the grounds of the Village Home at Barkingside.

What is it like to be an illegitimate child reared in a Barnardo home? Janet Hitchman spent two years of her childhood in the Barkingside home and describes the experience in her book *The King of the Barbareens.*[23] Janet Hitchman's mother died not long after her birth. Her father's name, which was different from her mother's surname, was scrawled on the back of the little girl's birth certificate, together with the date of his death in September 1916. He was perhaps killed on the Somme. Janet Hitchman, who was reared by a succession of foster parents and institutions, says that Barnardo, in her view, was the greatest philanthropist that England has ever known. Nevertheless, her opinion about the way in which the homes were run in the 1930s is not entirely uncritical. She draws attention to the fact that contact between children and their kin was often discouraged and, in some cases, positively obstructed. Letters coming into the home from parents or other relations were opened and read by the managers as a matter of course and were sometimes censored or even destroyed. Letters going out had to be submitted for inspection. Children whose parents or kinsfolk were criminal or otherwise unsuitable were still being hidden from them (by changes of name, for example) 40 years after the case of *Barnardo v. McHugh*.

The writer Frank Norman, who says that he is described in his Barnardo's file as 'the illegitimate son of an adventuress', was born in 1930 and spent the years between 1937 and 1946 in various Barnardo homes. His view of Barnardo's is much harsher than Janet Hitchman's. In his book *Banana Boy* he writes:

> How I hated it. . . . Why on Earth did they never ask me what I thought or felt? Why did they not bother to find out what kind of child I was? . . . I was utterly and completely starved of love.

> I think Barnardo's worst crime was their blatant underestimation of the intelligence of just about every boy and girl in their care. . . . The only trades that could be learnt at Goldings were carpentry, cobbling, gardening, tin-smithing and printing. . . . A boy with a creative streak in his make-up was a dead pigeon from the start.
>
> I do not entirely blame Barnardo's for the mental anguish of my childhood for no doubt the seeds were sown at birth. But their system only served to nurture my lamentable mental condition which manifested itself in violence, hate, and appalling loneliness, stemming from deep-rooted insecurity.[24]

Loneliness, insecurity, violent rages and strong self-hate are mentioned by both Hitchman and Norman as among the psychological problems which they believe to have been partly caused by childhood years spent in institutions. Should the reports of one or two (possibly unusual) individuals be taken too seriously? The empirical research of paediatricians (e.g. Harry Bakwin),[25] of psychotherapists (e.g. John Bowlby)[26] and of psychologists (e.g. A. M. McWhinnie, C. J. Adcock),[27] much of which after all, has to be based on personal reports and follow-ups, tends to support the general picture presented by illegitimate individuals, and by writers from Dickens to Frank Norman; as does common sense and the observation of ordinary people. It shows that the separation of an infant from its kin involves a variety of possible mental and physical hazards and confirms that on the whole children's homes and similar institutions are not good places in which to be reared.

Adoption

The advantages of adoption for an illegitimate child are fairly well-known and well-advertised, but since adoption is an officially approved policy the disadvantages are not very often discussed.

John Bowlby suggests that the aura of virtue that surrounds adoption is partly the result of sentimentality. He writes:

> instead of considering objectively what is best for the child and for the mother, workers of all kinds have too often been influenced by punitive and sentimental attitudes towards the

> errant mother. At one time the punitive attitude took the form of removing the baby from the mother as a punishment for her sins. Nowadays this punitive attitude seems to lead in the opposite direction and to insist that she should take full responsibility for caring for what she has so irresponsibly produced. . . . in a similar way sentimentalism can lead to either conclusion.[28]

Another related kind of sentimentality can be seen, perhaps, in the more or less official view that if a child is adopted young enough by 'the right' family, it is bound to fit into the family exactly as if it had been born into it. If the child is unhappy or if there is any strain, then someone or other must be at fault: a social worker for making a 'bad placing', or the adoptive family for being 'too strict' or 'too lax', or the child for having 'genetic problems'. But as there can be no such thing as a perfect family, or a perfect placing, or a perfect child, it might be a good idea to regard the happy fitting-in of an unrelated child as an ideal to be worked for rather than as something that can be taken for granted if only the social workers and adoption agencies could get things right.

Adopted people, in fact, often *feel different*. The organization Jigsaw, a now defunct pressure group whose purpose it was to make it easier for adopted people to trace their natural parents, gathered statements from adoptees on this matter. Here are some of them, which were quoted in a Jigsaw publication:[29]

> I had a very unhappy childhood with old 'parents' who never showed me any love. . . . I long for my real mother. . . . I pray that I will eventually find her.

> I am now 56 years old but have not lost the longing I have always had to find my real mother. . . .

> Despite being very fond of the three brothers who were born to my 'parents' after adopting me, I was different. The most obvious point was the fact that I looked so different. My personality was really very different too. I was boisterous, extrovert, friendly . . . whereas my brothers . . . were shy, introverted plodders, quiet and just like our parents. Very lovely people but too different from me to be able to cope with

me properly. . . . Other people who had themselves been adopted could tell that I was an adopted child, just as I could tell with other people. I don't know why, one just senses it.

Ever since I was small I've known that I was adopted and I have always taken a great interest in my natural parents, particularly my mother. My adoptive parents gave me all the information that they had but it just wasn't enough.

I was born illegitimately in 1945, fostered at eight weeks and legally adopted at four months. I had a very normal childhood, as far as I remember I was happy. . . . When I was ten years old I found out that I was adopted. . . . I felt utterly lost. Who am I? became the most compelling question in my life. . . . I soon learned that such questions should never be asked, they were painful for my 'parents', they showed a lack of gratitude in me, and finally, I couldn't by law be told. My identity, *mine*, was a state secret guarded with as much fear and embarrassment as nuclear waste. . . . I made many hopeless atempts to find my mother. . . . I remember an official at Somerset House in 1969 saying to me 'You're adopted – it's nothing to be ashamed of.' I said to him 'If it's nothing to be ashamed of, why all the secrecy?' [Eventually] I found my mother. . . . I feel reunited with myself. There are photographs of my grandparents, ancient stories of Uncle So-and-So and what he did. . . . there are my brothers and their lives. My own daughter suddenly has cousins.

My adoptive parents intended that I should never know that biologically I was not theirs. As far back as I can remember my relationship with them was badly strained. . . . my adoptive mother often voiced her disgust with unmarried mothers. . . . because I was physically unlike my adoptive parents, because I was told confusing accounts about my place of birth I grew up with the sense that there was some major secret somewhere. . . . Only at the age of 22 did I discover that I was indeed adopted. . . . it largely explained my adoptive parents' attitudes. . . . they must never have been able to come to terms with my illegitimacy and their own sterility and . . . feared that I would repeat my mother's 'badness'.

Jigsaw's comment on these and similar cases is as follows:

Many authorities on adoption would explain away [the] desire to find [the natural] mother as a product of an unhappy childhood in the adoptive home, or of not being told of the adoption itself so that the discovery comes as a shock . . . but adoptees in their hundreds stress over and over again that the desire to know their mother and discover the truth about their origins is a perfectly normal human need and is, in fact, a basic human right which has hitherto been denied them. This need to know is not a passing fad. It is not a rebellious teenagers' defiance or attempt to 'get back at' adoptive parents. It is a lifelong need. . . .

To be curious about one's biological mother and father is perfectly natural and in no way implies criticism of, or ingratitude to, adoptive parents. Our physical appearance and some aspects of health are genetically determined and will be passed on to our children. We all come from a long line of ancestors, there is a human need for continuity.[30]

On 12 November 1975 the law relating to adopted people's rights to access to their original birth record was changed. Until then an adopted person had no right in law to see his birth certificate, only the relevant entry in the Adopted Children Register. Pressure from adopted people and arguments marshalled by the organization Jigsaw led to a change in the law, so that now an adopted person of 18 years or more has a right in law to see his birth certificate. This means that adoptees can trace their biological mothers, but not vice versa, since the mother has no right in law to knowledge of her adopted child's whereabouts or new surname.

SOCIAL DISESTEEM AND OSTRACISM

The social disabilities of an illegitimate child are connected with those suffered by his mother. In the past, even the recent past – indeed, until about 1960 – the shame of being an unmarried mother was the worst possible shame a woman could suffer. The disgrace spread to all her immediate kin, who were expected to purge their shame by expelling the guilty woman from the family or by hiding her away somewhere. Secrecy about illegitimate birth was absolutely mandatory in normal families, as was shown by the custom of arranging for the baby to be born in a distant town or even a foreign country.

Moralizing has gradually gone out of fashion, but the psychologist tends to take over where the moralist leaves off. His punitive attitudes are less open than those of the moralist, hidden not only from the client but also from the psychologist himself. Unmarried mothers, and single mothers generally, are told by psychological experts that homes without a 'male presence' cause neurosis and homosexuality in children. Such experts frequently occupy positions of considerable authority – like priests in the Middle Ages – and no doubt succeed in terrifying many women.

In a talk which he gave in 1968 Dr Kenneth Soddy, consultant physician in the Department of Psychological Medicine at University College Hospital, said:

> quite a proportion of [unmarried] mothers . . . were motivated towards pregnancy for reasons which did not include loving a man. . . . let us be clear in our own minds that a woman who has no one for whose sake she is bringing up her child is operating from a position of psychological disadvantage. . . . I doubt if it is the answer, when pregnancy eventuates, to promise the girl an adequate allowance, with social welfare support. To do so may be unavoidable but I would question very seriously whether it is ever psychologically advantageous to entrust the upbringing of a baby or toddler to any woman who is not currently loved by a man for her own sake.[31]

Dr Soddy did not bother, in the course of a comparatively long talk, to produce one single piece of evidence in support of his thesis that a woman not currently loved by a man is not a fit person to care for her own child. The Director of the NCOPF wrote in 1974:

> one parent families suffer from a tendency to exaggerate the inherent emotional dangers faced by their children. . . . widespread beliefs about the inherent problems may affect the expectations of teachers and other people in contact with the child. Lone parents are very vulnerable to the views of others. We believe that the current negative attitudes to such families increases their chances of failure.[32]

One effect of disesteem and stigma can be to turn the mother and child against each other. Sometimes the children blame their mothers for giving them birth; thus, according to newspaper reports, Donald Hume, a convicted murderer, said that he hated many people, but most of all he hated his mother for having brought him into the world illegitimate. Fortunately, this is not the only possible reaction to the disesteem suffered by illegitimate people. Cyril Smith, MP for Rochdale, who is the illegitimate son of a charlady, seems to get on well with his mother; when he became mayor of Rochdale he made her his Lady Mayoress.[33]

In some parts of the world (e.g., in up-to-date circles in London) the stigma of bastardy has almost entirely vanished. Thus in an interview printed in a Sunday newspaper in 1981[34] the actress Jane Laportaire confessed quite cheerily to being the illegitimate daughter of an illegitimate mother, while the author Beryl Bainbridge, in an unconnected article on another page of the same issue, described her summer holiday in Corfu, saying casually in passing that her (unmarried) daughter, being pregnant at the time, had mostly sat on the beach and knitted. It is impossible to predict whether this change in attitude will be permanent or not. Could Nell Gwyn have predicted the activities of Dr Thomas Bowdler?

CHAPTER 9

Illegitimacy in Literature

Illegitimacy is a surprisingly common theme in literature. It appears in the Old Testament, in Classical literature, in Shakespeare, in Chaucer, in Restoration comedies and in large numbers of English, European and American novels of the eighteenth, nineteenth and twentieth centuries. In fact, ever since the novel was first invented novelists have been interested principally in the connected themes of love and marriage, seduction and illegitimacy. Authors who have written books in English which contain illegitimate characters include Jane Austen, Elizabeth Bowen, Charlotte Brontë, Agatha Christie, I. Compton-Burnett, Stephen Crane, Charles Dickens, Margaret Drabble, George du Maurier, George Eliot, Henry Fielding, E. M. Forster, Mrs Gaskell, Thomas Hardy, Nathaniel Hawthorne, Susan Hill, Henry Kingsley, D. H. Lawrence, George Meredith, Nancy Mitford, George Moore, Vladimir Nabokov, G. B. Shaw, Anthony Trollope and Oscar Wilde. Foreign authors who have treated the subject of illegitimacy include Eduardo Zamacois (a Cuban), Leo Tolstoy, Luigi Pirandello, Henrik Ibsen, Victor Hugo, Goethe, Fyodor Dostoyevsky, Anton Chekhov, Honoré de Balzac and J. Aho (a Finn) – and there are many, many more.

The reason why illegitimacy is a common theme is really rather simple. The main themes of fiction have always been love and death. Now, human sexual love has a good or noble side, and it also has a bad or dark side; and it is only natural that the dark side, as well as the good side, should appear in works of fiction, given the overall importance of love as a subject of art. The happier side of love is idealized in many plays and novels: it is represented by romantic attachment, chaste courtship, happy marriage, healthy, legitimate children and unproblematic inheritance. The darker side is all about seduction, rape, deception, prostitution, illegitimacy, social isolation, crime, poverty and disease.

Illegitimacy as a literary theme has many aspects. It is used by novelists as a contrast or backdrop to proper marriage, honour, respectability and security. It is one of the main subjects of ribaldry. The wicked bastard is an archetypal figure, a conveniently 'typical' villain who appears in many stories and plays. Illegitimacy itself is the paradigm of a shameful secret and can symbolize all kinds of other secrets, deceptions and mysteries. Illegitimacy is an obvious peg on which to hang a moral tale about sexual relationships. Finally, the illegitimate child or love child is quite often used by novelists as a symbol of natural goodness as opposed to worldly vanity and family greed.

RIBALDRY, PLEASANTRIES, 'META-RIBALDRY'

The dark, unhappy side of sexual love is the subject matter of a special kind of humour, namely, ribaldry. Ribaldry is, by definition, coarse and low, and its topics, by definition, are adultery, cuckolds, bastardy, impotence, veneral disease and so on. Of course, a certain centext is needed to make these things seem amusing, and certain conventions must be adhered to before it is quite proper to laugh about them. These conventions, in so far as they are literary, are exemplified in the music hall and in Restoration comedies.

A gentler kind of humour is also possible: since ribaldry is, by definition, coarse and low, not all pleasantries about sexual matters are necessarily ribald. An example of a non-ribald joke about bastardy occurs in Geoffrey Chaucer's *The Reeve's Tale*, where he pokes fun at village snobbery by attributing the elegance and social poise of the wife of the miller of Trumpington to the fact that she is the daughter of a celibate priest. Another good example of gentle humour about illegitimacy is Oscar Wilde's play *The Importance of Being Earnest*. This work, surely, is essentially a skit on the theme of the 'poor little nameless child'. The very title suggests as much, and the plot confirms the fact at many points. Thus in Act IV the hero leaps fallaciously to the conclusion that he is the illegitimate son of his old nurse, Miss Prism. Jack (or Earnest) has been abandoned in infancy by Miss Prism, the woman employed to look after him; intending to deposit the manuscript of her three-volume novel in the cloakroom of Victoria Station, she accidentally deposits the baby instead. Thus Jack becomes a foundling. He is reared by a benevolent guardian, who gives him a fictitious surname, Worthing, after the seaside resort. The name echoes the word 'worthy', of course, but also hints at the well-known fact that in the nineteenth century seaside resorts were traditionally the venues for extramarital affairs. Jack/Earnest grows up into an English gentleman, with a gentleman's income inherited from his guardian, but when he falls in love and wants to marry he is confronted with difficulties. The difficulties are mainly hilarious variants of the disabilities of namelessness (bastardy). Quizzed by Lady Bracknell, his prospective mother-in-law, Jack has to confess that he does not know the identity of his father or mother, to which Lady Bracknell makes the famous riposte:

> To lose one parent, Mr Worthing, may be regarded as a misfortune; to lose both looks like carelessness.[1]

Jack further confesses that when found by his guardian, he was inside 'a somewhat large black leather handbag, with handles to it', which information provokes from Lady Bracknell the comment:

> to be born, or at any rate bred, in a handbag, whether it had handles or not, seems to me to display a contempt for the ordinary decencies of family life that reminds one of the worst excesses of the French Revolution.[2]

She advises Jack

> to try and acquire some relations as soon as possible, and to make a definite effort to produce at any rate one parent, of either sex, before the season is over.[3]

For, as she rightly emphasizes,

> You can hardly imagine that I and Lord Bracknell would

dream of allowing our only daughter – a girl brought up with the utmost care – to marry into a cloakroom, and form an alliance with a parcel.[4]

I define 'meta-ribaldry' as jokes about ribaldry. There is a good example of this comparatively rare genre on a gramophone record made by Peter Cook and Dudley Moore. In one sketch two characters called Pete and Dud, overgrown adolescents or retarded adults, reminisce about their schooldays and about a school friend by the name of Roger Old-Clever-Drawers Braintree:

Pete: . . . he come up to me and told me, 'I've discovered the most disgusting word in the world. It's so filthy that no one's allowed to see it except bishops, and nobody knows what it means.'
Dud: What was the word, Pete?
Pete: Well, he wouldn't tell me. I had to give him half a pound of peppermints before he'd let it out.
Dud: But what *was* the word, Pete?
Pete: (*hushed*) Bastard.
(*Pause*)
Dud: (*casually*) What's it mean, Pete?
Pete: [*explains how he looked the word up in a dictionary in a public library*] . . . And there was the word in all its horror: 'Bastard = child born out of wedlock.'
Dud: (*mystified but pretending to feel disgusted*) *Ughhhh*! (*Pause*) But what's a wedlock, Pete?
Pete: It's a terrible thing, Dud. It's a sort of cross between a steam-engine and a padlock.[5]

CONTRASTS

Many writers, particularly novelists, contrast the good with the bad sides of sexual love – they contrast, that is to say, honour and shame, legitimacy and illegitimacy, poverty and inheritance, marriage and seduction, disease and purity and so on. Such comparisons can develop into amazingly savage denunciations of institutions or individuals: consider, for example, Charles Dickens's description of one of the Founding Fathers of the USA: 'He dreamed of Freedom in a slave's embrace, and waking sold her offspring and his own in public markets.'[6] In *King Lear* Shakespeare contrasts the excellent behaviour of the Duke of Gloucester's legitimate son Edgar with the bad behaviour of his bastard half-brother Edmund.[7] In Daniel Defoe's novel *Moll Flanders* the author compares the respectable (married) phases of the heroine's life with the disreputable (unmarried) phases. In more than one of her novels Jane Austen contrasts the happiness of a heroine whose sensible behaviour leads to marriage with the sorry fate of a female eloper whose innocence, stupidity or fecklessness inevitably results in an illegitimate baby or a disgraceful forced wedding. In Dickens's masterpiece *Bleak House* the life story of the illegitimate and penniless heroine, Esther Summerson, is intricately interwoven with the separate tale of the Jarndyce inheritance lost in Chancery. In Anthony Trollope's novels *Ralph the Heir* and *Dr Thorne* money and legitimacy and illegitimacy are the main themes, which make up a see-saw of possibilities and contrasts.

THE ARCHETYPAL BASTARD

Primary qualities

In ordinary usage, as we have remarked, the word 'bastard' is a term of abuse, almost a swear word. The word is used insultingly and metaphorically much more often than it is used literally. This can only be explained by reference to beliefs once widely held about illegitimate people. Such beliefs are presumably as old as the institution of marriage itself. Be that as it may, hostile feelings about bastards and the belief that they are generally very bad people find expression in very ancient archetypes.

Thus in old histories and legends the sons of kings and of slave girls appear as usurpers and murderers. The reason is perhaps not far to seek: if such men did not become usurpers, they would remain slaves, nameless and invisible; they would not appear in the pages of history at all.

Plato tells a story about an usurper in the dialogue *Gorgias*. In that work Polus is made to relate the history of Archelaus, ruler of Macedonia. Archelaus' father was a king, Perdiccas, and his mother was a slave girl who belonged to Alcetas, the brother of Perdiccas. After the death of his father, Archelaus kills his uncle and master, Alcetas, then murders Alcetas' son Alexander, and finally does away with Perdiccas' legitimate heir, a boy of seven whom he thrusts down a well. By these means he becomes king himself. Polus remarks to Socrates: 'he had no claim to the power he now enjoys for he was by rights the slave of Alcetas.'[8]

There is a somewhat similar tale in the Old Testament. In Judges the tale is told of Gideon:

> Gideon had threescore and ten sons of his body begotten: for he had many wives.
>
> And his concubine that was in Shechem, she also bare him a son, whose name he called Abimelech.[9]

After the death of Gideon, whose other name was Jerubbaal,

> Abimelech hired vain and light persons, which followed him.
>
> And he went unto his father's house at Ophrah, and slew his brethren the sons of Jerubbaal, being threescore and ten persons, upon one stone. . . .[10]

In this way Abimelech became the ruler of the Shechemites. (He was killed a few years later by a woman who dropped a millstone on his head from the top of a tower during a siege.)

Archelaus and Abimelech could perhaps be best described as legendary 'proto-bastards'.

The bastard as usurper and murderer is an archetype and, as such, appears over and over again in European literature and the literature of the English-speaking world. Faulconbridge in Shakespeare's *King John* and Edmund of *King Lear* are striking examples – characteristic bastards. In Dostoyevsky's novel *The Brothers Karamazov* old Karamazov's bastard son, Smerdyakov, is a parricide. As well as that, he commits suicide. Aeneas Manson, the illegitimate villain of Thomas Hardy's novel *Desperate Remedies*, is a murderer and a suicide. Manolo, the adulterine bastard in Zamacois's story *Their Son*, beats up his mother and kills his step-father.

Parricide, murder and usurpation are the primary qualities of fictional bastards, but fictional bastards also have secondary qualities, and these too show what our ancestors thought about illegitimate people.

Secondary qualities

Bastards in books are often tainted with diseases or deformity; they also suffer from such disabilities as alcoholism, drug addiction and violent, uncontrollable rages.

Caliban, the monster in Shakespeare's *The Tempest*, is a bastard.[11] In Ibsen's play *The Wild Duck* the illegitimate girl Hedwig is threatened with blindness, inherited from her natural father. Smerdyakov, the villain of *The Brothers Karamazov* is an epileptic; he is also said to be wizened, yellow and emasculate. The main character of the story *Outlawed*, by the Finnish author Aho, suffers from blind, uncontrollable rages, and, like many real and fictional illegitimate people, he ends up in prison. In Nathaniel Hawthorne's celebrated novel *The Scarlet Letter* the illegitimate girl Pearl is said to be an imp, and it is suggested that she is non-human.[12] The hero of Pirandello's story *In Silence*, which is about two illegitimate brothers, is short-sighted, weak, clumsy and nervous, and ends up killing himself and his baby brother.

Diseases and deformities stand in part for punishment, but they also express the idea that bastards, because they are not members of proper families, are not proper members of the human family. They are tainted, monstrous, incomplete, betwixt-and-betweens, mongrels – a different kind of animal from *us*. Addictions and rages, on the other hand, symbolize the sexual uncontrol of the parents. The lawless act generates a lawless being.

In books bastards often have a fragile hold on life. They are the victims of murders, or else they tend to be self-destructive or to undergo mysterious accidents. Such fictional events no doubt reflect reality to some extent, but they also represent the judgement that these people ought never to have been born in the first place; they ought not to exist at all. We find that infancticide is an extremely common fate for illegitimate babies in books. There is room for only a few examples.

In *Henry VI, Part I*, Warwick says to the (supposedly pregnant) Joan of Arc: 'we'll have no bastards live.'[13] Then he puts her to death. In *The Winter's Tale* Leontes rejects the infant Perdita:

> This brat is none of mine;
> It is the issue of Polixenes:
> Hence with it; and, together with the dam,
> Commit them to the fire![14]

(Luckily, these two escape.) Goethe's version of the Faust legend centres on Faust's seduction of Marguerite, the consequences of which include the birth of a baby, Marguerite's murder of the child and her final execution. Janácek's opera *Jenufa* is about the murder of an illegitimate baby who is done away with so that its mother can marry and acquire respectability. In a film made in China in the 1950s called *The White-Haired Girl* the heroine drowns her new-born baby (product of the landlord's lust) before running away to join the Long March. And in 1971 the young British author Susan Hill published a short story called *Somerville* which returns to the ancient theme of illegitimacy and infanticide. The reader will no doubt be able to recollect many other stories, plays and legends in which the killing of an unwanted infant is part of the plot.

TRUTH AND FALSEHOOD, MORALITY AND IMMORALITY

Illegitimacy is the paradigmatic skeleton in the cupboard, a secret far more shameful than bankruptcy, insanity or any crime. As such, it makes a very suitable subject for an author who wishes to discuss truth and falsity, or fraud and honesty, or mysteries and revelations. Thus in many stories it appears both in its own right, as it were, and also as a symbol for something else. It appears as a simple secret in detective stories and mystery stories, and as something more complicated in moral tales and in 'philosophical' plays and novels about truthfulness, hypocrisy or sexual morality. Ibsen's play *The Wild Duck*, for instance, is about the discovery of secret illegitimacy, but it is also about the nature of self-deception, the value of truth, the dangers of hypocrisy and deceit.

As well as writing *The Importance of Being Earnest*, which,

I have argued, is a skit on the theme of the 'poor little nameless child', Oscar Wilde also attempted a serious play about illegitimacy, *A Woman of No Importance*. The plot of this drama, or melodrama, is in some ways very similar to the plot of G. B. Shaw's play *Mrs Warren's Profession*. Both plays begin with a situation in which a well-off, middle-aged woman (Mrs Arbuthnot, Mrs Warren) enters or re-enters fashionable society after an unexplained period of absence or seclusion. Then, in a scene of dramatic revelation, the woman's child (Gerald Arbuthnot, Vivie Warren) is told of his or her illegitimacy and of the mother's scandalous, sinful past. Tainted money is offered to the young hero and heroine: Vivie is offered her mother's fortune, based on investment in brothels; Gerald is offered a job, travel, a career, houses and land by his natural father, the cynical seducer Lord Illingworth. Vivie refuses the fortune and cuts herself off from her mother; Gerald refuses the job, lands, etc. and cuts himself off from his father. But Vivie is able to support herself by becoming an accountant, and Gerald has the good luck to marry an American heiress.

A Woman of No Importance, first staged in 1893, was greeted by the audience 'with thunderous applause'.[15] *Mrs Warren's Profession*, written in 1894, was banned by the Lord Chamberlain and was not publicly performed until after the First World War. In 1902, however, a theatre club, the Stage Society, gave a private performance of the play, to which the critics were invited. Shaw described the occasion thus:

> No author who has ever known the exultation of sending the Press into an hysterical tumult of protest, of moral panic, of involuntary and frantic confession of sin, of a horror of conscience in which the power of distinguishing between the work of art on the stage and the real life of the spectator is confused and overwhelmed, will ever care for the stereotyped compliments which every successful farce or melodrama elicits from the newspapers. . . . What a triumph for the actor . . . to reduce a jaded London journalist to the condition of the simple sailor in the Wapping gallery who shouts execrations at Iago and warnings to Othello. . .![16]

Why this 'tumult of protest' and 'moral panic'? Well, in spite of similarities of plot, the moral message of *Mrs Warren's*

Profession is quite different from that of *A Woman of No Importance*. Mrs Arbuthnot says things like, 'We are among the outcasts. . . .', 'I drag a heavy chain. . . .', 'I am a tainted thing. . . .' and 'Child of my shame, be still the child of my shame!' The moral message, such as it is, seems to be that both men and women are to be blamed for the results of lust and promiscuity, but that it is probably as well to forgive and forget. Mrs Warren, on the other hand, says things like, '[A whorehouse] is a much better place for a woman to be in than the white-lead factory. . . .' and 'Of course, [prostitution] is worthwhile to a poor girl. . . . It's far better than any other opportunity open to her. I've always thought that oughtn't to be. . . . but it's so, right or wrong. . . .' The moral message, says Shaw, is twofold:

> Prostitution is caused not by female depravity and male licentiousness, but simply by underpaying, undervaluing, and overworking women so shamefully that the poorest of them are forced to resort to it to keep body and soul together. . . .[17]

and:

> [The fact is] that the children of any polyandrous group will, when they grow up, inevitably be confronted, as those of Mrs Warren's group are in my play, with the insoluble problem of their own consanguinity.[18]

Evidently Shaw's moral message was acceptable neither to the Lord Chamberlain nor to the Press critics.

THE LOVE CHILD

The archetype of the wicked, weak or diseased bastard is not yet defunct: authors who would scorn the ploy of making a bastard character into a villain sometimes fall victim to the opposite temptation and make their villains into bastards. (Vladimir Nabokov, for instance, does this in a short story called *Tyrants Destroyed*.) On the other hand, there are several writers who set out deliberately to overturn traditional ideas about illegitimate people. Such authors represent the illegitimate individual as a victim and not as a villain. Two considerable examples are Victor Hugo in his long novel *Les Misérables*, and Charles Dickens in *Oliver Twist* and *Bleak*

House. The hero of *Oliver Twist* is technically illegitimate but, as it were, ideologically legitimate. He is the innocent victim of family greed – which forced his father to marry a woman he did not love – and of the machinations of a scoundrelly half-brother who wishes to destroy him. The half-brother, Edward Leeford, alias Monks, is technically legitimate but, as it were, ideologically illegitimate. Like a real bastard, he is a person about whose surname there is some doubt; furthermore, he is archetypally degenerate, diseased in body and in will. At the end of the story Edward Leeford is expelled from the family and Oliver, the hero, is welcomed into it. Dickens thus reverses the traditional roles of legitimate and illegitimate characters in his story – with the clear intention of attacking the ancient dictum that tells us all bastards are bad. Esther Summerson, the heroine and narrator of *Bleak House*, is also ideologically legitimate, being almost unbearably good, even by Dickensian standards.

A new archetype appears in fiction, therefore, which can perhaps be traced back to Victor Hugo and Charles Dickens – the archetype of the love child. There are many twentieth-century examples, including Stephen Wonham in E. M. Forster's *The Longest Journey*, the child Leopold in Elizabeth Bowen's *The House in Paris*, Esther's son in George Moore's novel *Esther Waters* and the baby Olivia in Margaret Drabble's book *The Millstone*. The love child, if female, is beautiful, delicate and other-worldly; if male, then manly, straightforward, truthful, natural. The love child represents nature as opposed to convention, true love as opposed to wordly marriage and spiritual values as opposed to material inheritance.

THE FICTIONAL 'CRYPTO-BASTARD'

Finally, we may mention briefly the fictional 'crypto-bastard', or legitimate foundling, the character (encountered mainly in Victorian novels) who in real life would almost certainly be illegitimate but who has been supplied, often very improbably, with a pair of married parents by his or her authorial creator. The improbable legitimacy of the fictional crypto-bastard is not always central to a plot – e.g., a plot about a mysterious inheritance – but may be necessary purely and simply because of the *goodness* of the character – necessary, that is, because of the author's wish to avoid Dickensian political and social argumentation on the one hand and, on the other, because of his need to keep his hero or heroine clear of taint. A good example of this kind of character is Eppie in George Eliot's novel *Silas Marner*. Before the novel begins (we are asked to suppose) Eppie's father, a gentleman, has actually *married* a drunken, drug-addicted barmaid, who subsequently runs away, then gives birth to Eppie, then leaves the baby in a cottage, then dies. Since Eppie is legitimate, no argument is needed to prove to the reader that she will not necessarily inherit her mother's wickedness: the novelist needs only to depict the heroine as good, not to prove that she can be.

CHAPTER 10

Religion

Secular law on marriage and related matters is historically founded on religious law. In Europe secular law is a modification and elaboration of Roman law, Christianity and Judaism. In the Middle East and much of Africa laws about marriage, legitimacy and inheritance are based on various interpretations of the Koran.

JUDAISM

Traditional Jewish law regards God as the source of all law. It is based on the Bible, on the Talmud and on other rabbinical teachings and interpretations. Marriage law and the traditional marriage ceremonies are essentially religious in character. The law of the state of Israel follows traditional law in many aspects, but especially in matters connected with marriage, the family and sexual morality; however, its punishments for law breakers are not biblically severe.

God's first commandment to man was: 'Be fruitful, and multiply, and replenish the earth. . . .'[1] Marriage is regarded not only as normal but also as normally required. Rabbinical teaching is that on the Day of Judgement every man will be asked 'Did you marry? Did you found a family?'[2] Jewish sayings about marriage include 'A man's wife is his home', 'A wifeless man is not a man', 'A childless man is one of the living dead.'[3] The ideal child is religious and attends religious school (i.e., he is a son), and a man with sons is seen as having been blessed by God.

Various types of marriage are prohibited. Incestuous marriages, as defined in Leviticus, are void from the start, as are adulterous marriages and marriages between Jews and (unconverted) non-Jews. Other prohibited marriages are unlawful but valid: the fact that one's marriage is prohibited, though valid, is a ground for divorce. Prohibited marriages include the marriage of a priest (i.e. a man descended from Aaron and belonging to the tribe of Levi) to a woman who is a convert or a divorcée; the marriage of a priest to a harlot; the marriage of a priest to a woman who is herself the child of an illicit priestly marriage; the marriage of the High Priest to a widow or to any women forbidden to any priest as listed above; the marriage of any Jewish man to a woman who he has married before and who has been married to someone else in the interim (cf. Muslim law cited on p. 148); the marriage of a woman divorced for adultery to her partner in adultery. Polygamy is not forbidden in the Old Testament, but it has been prohibited for Ashkenazy Jews since the eleventh century. In 1950 a national rabbinical conference held in Israel stipulated that monogamy must be the only form of marriage lawful for Jews living in Israel.[4] Traditional thinking on concubinage is not unanimous. Some say that concubinage is forbidden in the Bible: 'There shall be no whore of the daughters of Israel, nor a sodomite of the sons of Israel.'[5] Others distinguish between whores, or harlots, and concubines, arguing that the concubine is faithful to one man and is not the kind of girl referred to in the text quoted above. However, it is agreed that concubinage is forbidden by rabbinical teaching.

Two ceremonies are needed for a traditional Jewish marriage, the first stage being a kind of betrothal, the second the start of married life. In modern times both ceremonies take place on the same day. In the first ceremony the groom gives the bride a gold ring and says, 'Behold, thou art consercrated to me by this ring according to the Law of Moses and Israel.' He must then agree in writing to accept the obligations and duties of a 'Jewish husband'. In the second ceremony blessings are followed by the ritual isolation of the bride and groom, which in modern times is carried out symbolically and consists of their standing together under a wedding canopy. A Jewish husband has ten obligations and four rights. He is obliged to provide his wife with sustenance, to supply her with clothing and lodging, to cohabit with her, to provide her with money as agreed in writing, to procure medical attention when she is ill, to ransom her if she is taken captive, to provide suitable burial for her if she dies, to provide for her maintenance after his own death (this includes ensuring her right to remain in his house as his widow), to provide for the support of their unmarried daughters after his death, and to ensure that their sons inherit their mother's money.[6] The father's own money and other property is automatically inherited by his sons under traditional law; the law of the state of Israel, however, differs from tradition here and allows widows and daughters to inherit as well as sons.[7] The four traditional rights of a Jewish husband are to benefit from his wife's housework and handiwork, to use her chance finds or gains, to use and enjoy the advantages of her property, and to inherit her estate.

A man must maintain his children, both legitimate and illegitimate: a woman has no duty of maintenance under traditional law. Custody of children depends on age and sex; daughters stay with the mother always, boys until they are six, after which the father has custody. Unless both parents are Jewish, the father has no legal standing under Jewish law in regard to his children – no duty of maintenance and no right of custody.[8] Adoption is not recognized in traditional law; the state of Israel, however, passed an Adoption Act in 1960.[9]

An individual cannot appoint heirs because his heirs are predetermined by the law: Jews in the Diaspora made wills, of course, so as to ensure the rights of their heirs under the civil law of the country in which they were living. Israel today has a law on inheritance which follows tradition in some respects and diverges from it in others. The main difference is that modern law allows women to inherit as well as men, and one of the main similarities is that the illegitimate child has the same rights of inheritance as the legitimate child. Questions of lineage, though, depend on the type of illegitimacy involved, as described below. Under the old law a man's property was divided among his sons at his death; the first-born son received a double share and the other sons equal shares.

Divorce is permitted under Jewish law. The justification is taken from Scripture:

> When a man hath taken a wife, and married her, and it come to pass that she find no favour in his eyes, because he hath found some uncleanness in her: then let him write her a bill of divorcement, and give it in her hand, and send her out of his house.[10]

A rabbinical enactment forbade the husband to divorce his wife against her will: this led to the development of the idea that divorce is a mutual agreement between the parties to the marriage and not the act of a court. The role of the courts, therefore, is to decide the question of whether, and in what circumstances, one or other party may be compelled to give or receive a bill of divorcement. Divorce by mutual consent is therefore the basic type of divorce, but there are also many situations in which one or other party may demand a divorce: these situations include the contraction of contagious disease (such as leprosy), impotence, the sterility of either party (proved by ten years of childlessness) and bad conduct such as 'unceasing quarrels', serious infidelity, assault, irreligious behaviour, apostasy.[11]

In the state of Israel divorce is handled by the rabbinical courts. Marriage too is a wholly religious matter in modern Israel, which has no civil marriage as such. All Jews in Israel must marry according to Jewish religious law. This includes Jews who are visitors but who want to marry in Israel. Christian citizens must marry according to Christian religious law, and Muslim citizens must marry according to Muslim law. Outside the state of Israel a Jew who wishes to marry a Gentile cannot marry in a synagogue, nor will a rabbi take any part in the ceremony: in other words, mixed marriages between Jews and unconverted non-Jews are unlawful. On the other hand, the state of Israel contains in its criminal code no punishments for mixed marriages, and its law of succession provides that differences of religion do not affect rights of inheritance.[12] Although mixed marriages are prohibited, the child of a mixed marriage is not necessarily illegitimate: its legitimacy will depend on other considerations.

Jewish traditional law on legitimacy and illegitimacy is strongly affected by the endogamous character of Jewish marriage law and by the importance accorded to genealogy and pedigree. The importance of genealogy goes back to the very beginning of Jewish history (see, for example, the Book of Numbers and the Book of Ezra). The Jews, of course, are patrilineal, thus the lineage of the individual, the identity of the individual within the larger tribe, depends on the identity of his father. Nevertheless, the individual cannot belong to the larger tribe at all – that is, he does not count as a Jew – unless his mother is a born or converted Jewess.

In Scripture it is stated: 'A bastard shall not enter into the congregation of the Lord; even to his tenth generation shall he not enter into the congregation of the Lord'[13] – which is to say that a bastard is not a Jew or Jewess and hence may not marry a Jew or Jewess. It follows that the descendants of a bastard cannot be Jews either. But a bastard (*mamzer*) is not a child born out of wedlock: this is not the definition under Jewish law.

Jewish law distinguishes four categories of offspring: children of parents who are married to each other; children of parents who are not married to each other; children of parents only one of whom is Jewish; and children whose parentage is not known. Any of these four kinds of offspring can be either legitimate or bastards, according to the prescriptions listed below.[14]

1. (a) Children of parents married to each other in a valid and non-prohibited marriage are incontestably legitimate. They take the status of the father and belong to his lineage: thus if the father is a priest (i.e., is descended from Aaron and belongs to the tribe of Levi), the son will be too: if the mother is a priest's daughter and the father an ordinary Jew, the child will be an ordinary Jew.
   (b) Children of parents whose marriage is valid but prohibited take the status of the 'tainted' parent. Thus if one parent is a *mamzer(et)*, the child will be a bastard also. Again, since a marriage between a priest and a divorcée is prohibited, the son of such a marriage cannot be a priest himself and will be called *halal* (profaned). A *halal* is a Jew – i.e., not a *mamzer*.
2. The child of an unmarried mother is not illegitimate *per se*, but its paternity must be established before its status can be. Onus of proof of paternity is on the child (or its mother).

(a) If at the time of conception there was no legal bar to the marriage of the parents, and if paternity is proved, the status of the child is determined in the same way as the status of the children of married parents.

(b) If the parents could not have contracted a valid marriage (i.e., if their marriage would have been not only legally but also biblically prohibited because incestuous or adulterous) then the child is a *mamzer(et)*.

3. When only one parent is Jewish the rule is that the child takes the mother's status. Hence the child of a non-Jew and a legitimate (non-*mamzeret*) Jewess is a legitimate Jew, subject to the limitation that such a child, if female, cannot marry a priest. The child of a non-Jew and a *mamzeret* woman (a bastard woman of Jewish blood) is itself a *mamzer*. The child of a legitimate Jewish man and a non-Jewish mother is not a Jew but may become a convert, like any other non-Jew: the legitimacy or otherwise of its mother under some other, non-Jewish law, will not affect its status. The child of a non-Jewish mother and a *mamzer* (a man who is illegitimate but of Jewish blood) is not itself Jewish and is therefore not a *mamzer*, even though its father is. Such a child can also become a convert, like any other non-Jew.
4. A child whose parentage is unknown is called *asufi* (foundling) or *shetuki* (undisclosed). The first is a child found abandoned and whose parents are both unknown. It is obviously not possible to ascertain whether or not such a child is Jewish, apart from circumstantial evidence (e.g., circumcision), or whether its parents were themselves *mamzerim*. Thus the child is initially regarded as a doubtful or possible *mamzer* and also as a doubtful or possible Gentile. Circumstances are taken to resolve the doubt in certain cases – for example, if the child has been abandoned in a synagogue, it is assumed that the parents were proper non-*mamzer* Jews forced by circumstances to give up their infant. A *shetuki* is the child of a Jewish unmarried mother who will not or cannot say who its father is. Again, its Jewishness and its legitimacy must depend, in the end, on whatever evidence crops up about its paternity. If the mother is prepared to declare that the father was either

legitimate (non-*mamzer*) or Gentile, then the child will be legitimate and Jewish, since it has a Jewish mother.

Traditional Jewish law frowns upon celibacy, and the priesthood is not supposed to be celibate. Every Jew, ideally, is supposed to marry, and traditional teaching urges both men and women to marry young, men at about 20 if possible. As has already been noted, the marriage rules for priests are stricter than the general marriage rules. A 'blemished' man, even if a Levite, was disqualified from officiating in the Temple. 'Blemishes' which disqualified included castration, loss of voice and being too young. Moral and religious 'blemishes' also disqualified: thus a man who had committed adultery, or homicide, or idolatry, for example, would be disqualified. A man born of an unlawful marriage would also be disqualified, while still possibly counting as a member of the priestly tribe. A man born of incestuous or adulterous union or of an illicit priestly marriage was disqualified by virtue of his exclusion from the proper lineage.

Orthodox Jews adhere to traditional teaching on marriage and related matters. Reform Jews accept some parts of the teaching and reject other parts, with variation between different communities and different synagogues.

CHRISTIANITY

The general rules about marriage and legitimacy in Christendom are described in chapter 3. To these we may add some remarks on Roman Catholic teaching on marriage and legitimacy.

The teachings of the Roman Catholic Church are founded on Scripture and on the 'traditions of the Church'. The 'traditions' include the decrees of the Councils of the Church, the papal decrees, the judgements of the Offices of the Holy See and the codification of all these in canon law.

Catholic teaching is that God is the fount and source of all law, and that He establishes the foundations of legal systems through the natural (moral) law and through divine, positive law, which is ultimately to be located in the New Testament, in the life of Christ, His miracles, His parables and other teachings and so on. Human legislators act by virtue of the power or authority given them by God.

The history of canon law begins with the Acts of the Apostles and the writings of the Fathers of the Church. The Oriental Councils of the Church issued decrees which are mentioned in the acts of the Council of Chalcedon (AD 451). Two so-called Latin collections, made in Spain and Italy in the late fifth and early sixth century respectively, incorporate the earlier decrees, together with decrees from some Western Councils. The Scythian monk, Denis the Little, made a collection of canons in the sixth century which were accepted as authoritative by the Synod of Aix-la-Chapelle in 802. It contained 50 apostolic canons of the Oriental Councils, 138 canons from the Council of Carthage of 419 and 38 decrees of various popes from 385 to 498. Subsequently compilations were made by Abbo, Abbot of Fleury (d. 1004), Burchard, Bishop of Worms (d. 1023), Anselm, Bishop of Lucca (d. 1086) and Ivo, Bishop of Chartres (d. 1117). Between 1140 and 1150 Gratian, a Camaldolese monk, made a collection of all the canons, since named the *Decretum Magistri Gratiani*, which superseded all previous collections. The *Decretals of Pope Gregory IX*, issued in 1234, incorporated Gratian's canons and added others. These works, together with revisions and supplementary books added by Pope Boniface IX, Pope Clement V and Pope John XXII, were collected together by Pope Gregory XIII (1572–85) into a work (or, rather, a library) called the *Corpus Juris Canonici.* Since then the decrees of councils and popes issued in the last 400 years have appeared in incomplete additional collections. In 1917–18 the *Codex Juris Canonici* was promulgated, consisting of 2414 canons; it was based on all the former works and was drawn up in Rome by a commission of cardinals and canonists.[15]

Roman Catholic teaching on marriage and related matters is also to be found in decrees issued since 1918; for example, the encyclicals 'Christian Marriage' (Pope Pius XI, 1930) and 'On Human Life' (Pope Paul VI, 1968), and the Apostolic Letter 'Mixed Marriage' (Pope Paul VI, 1970).[16]

Marriage is not commanded by the Roman Catholic Church, nor even recommended, except for the human race as a whole. In the New Testament the individual is urged to opt for celibacy.[17] Marriage is not actually condemned, however. Marriage between baptized persons is both a sacrament and a contract: marriage between persons neither of whom is baptized is merely a contract. As a contract, marriage gives a man and a woman a perpetual, mutual and exclusive right to the body of the other for procreative acts. It is a unique contract in that it has a divine origin in the law of nature. The right to marry is common to all; this means that every normal adult has a right to make a first marriage. It is possible for the authorities in Rome to forbid a man or woman to make a second marriage (for example, after the annulment of a marriage). The primary purpose of marriage is the generation of children; the secondary purpose is the mutual aid of the partners. Those who have the power and the right to beget a child have the power and the right to educate it.[18] A non-Catholic begetter, however, if married to a Catholic, must promise to allow the children of the marriage to be educated as (and therefore by) Catholics. Some authorities say[19] that a marriage can be licitly contracted for either of its two main purposes: thus, it would seem, marriages between people who cannot have children are alright. The Roman Catholic Church does not, in fact, forbid marriage between elderly men and women; impotent men are not supposed to marry, however.

Marriage has a sacred and religious character, such that even unbelievers are bound to take note of its essential properties: unity and indissolubility. So unbelievers who form contracts for the purpose of procreation ought to, even if they do not, regard those contracts as monogamous and indissoluble.

Roman Catholicism does not allow divorce, of course. However marriages may be ended by annulment or by dispensation. But 'dispensation does not abrogate the law.' Current Roman Catholic doctrine enshrines the following seven prescriptions:[20]

1. A marriage between two baptized persons that is contracted with the intention of procreation and consummated by sexual intercourse cannot be dissolved by any authority on earth.
2. A marriage between two baptized persons who, by mutual

vows or agreement, do not consummate the marriage can be dissolved by religious profession or by papal dispensation.

3. A marriage between two baptized persons that is contracted with the intention of procreation, but for some reason is not consummated by sexual intercourse, can be dissolved by religious profession or by papal dispensation.
4. A marriage contracted by two baptized persons with no intention to procreate, which is consummated by sexual intercourse, can be judged by the courts of the Roman Curia to be either indissoluble (i.e., it is deemed to be a real marriage) or invalid (i.e., it is deemed to be not a marriage but concubinage), according to the particular circumstances.
5. A marriage between two baptized persons who intend that it shall be impermanent or who assume that it will be impermanent, which is consummated by sexual intercourse, might be judged by the courts of the Roman Curia to be either indissoluble (because it is deemed to be a real marriage) or invalid, depending on circumstances.
6. A marriage contracted (after dispensation) between a baptized and an unbaptized person with the intention of procreation, which is consummated by sexual intercourse, is dissoluble without dispensation in somewhat the same circumstances (e.g., desertion) as would allow for a civil divorce.
7. A marriage between two unbaptized persons with the intention of procreation that is consummated by sexual intercourse is dissoluble if one partner is converted to the Christian faith, is baptized and then wants to end the marriage. This, the so-called Pauline Privilege, stems from St Paul's First Letter to the Corinthians.[21] The dissolution can be effected (if the case is clear) by a bishop, but the Holy See can be asked to rule on difficult cases.

The use of the Pauline Privilege as a lawful method of ending marriage dates from the fourth century; the dissolution of non-consummated marriages for religious reasons dates from the eleventh century; the dissolution of non-consummated marriages by papal dispensation dates from Pope Martin V

(1417–31); the dissolution of non-sacramental unions dates from the sixteenth century; and the dissolution of marriages between the baptized and the unbaptized was explicitly recognized as lawful in 1924.[22]

A marriage between a Roman Catholic and a baptized non-Roman Catholic needs a dispensation from the impediment of mixed religion. A marriage between a Roman Catholic and non-baptized person needs a dispensation from the impediment of disparity of cult. As we have noted 'dispensation does not abrogate the law'; thus good reasons, of a special not a general nature, are always needed for the granting of a dispensation. According to some modern authorities, the following considerations should be taken into account: the danger of a Roman Catholic's contracting a Protestant or civil marriage should be avoided if possible; invalid marriages should be validated, where possible, for the spiritual good of the parties; children already born should be legitimated if possible; the hope of the conversion of a non-Roman Catholic partner must be taken into consideration. Further, the scarcity or lack of suitable Roman Catholic marriage partners in the community can be a reason for dispensation, as can illicit pregnancy. Canon 2319 states that Roman Catholics who marry before a non-Roman Catholic priest, or who have their children baptized by a non-Roman Catholic priest, or who have their children educated by ministers of non-Roman Catholic sects are excommunicated automatically, but Pope Paul VI retroactively abrogated this canon in 1970.[23]

The Roman Catholic Church distinguishes between two kinds of illegitimate children: natural children and spurious children. Natural children are those born to unmarried partners who could have married but did not; spurious children (*ex damnato coitu*) are born of adultery, or incest, or sacrilegeous union. The Church also distinguishes between two types of legitimation. One type renders legitimate a child who was formerly illegitimate. This can happen through the subsequent marriage of parents, or by a dispensation which allows the parents to marry or to count their union as a marriage proper, or as a favour granted by the Holy See. A child legitimated thus has a juridical status similar to, but not identical with, that of a legitimate child, according to canon law. The second kind of legitimation is retroactive and makes a child legitimate from the time of its birth. This happens when the unlawful or invalid marriage of its parents is granted sanation, a proceeding which retroactively renders the marriage valid and lawful. A child legitimated in this way is fully legitimate.[24]

The celibacy of the priesthood is justified by reference to the New Testament, especially the words of St Paul. Early Christians regarded celibacy as the summit of human perfection but did not treat it as compulsory for clergy. The idea that the clergy ought to be celibate is thought to date from the fourth century. The Roman Council of 386 enacted a law ordaining celibacy for certain clergy, which was confirmed by Pope Leo the Great in the fifth century and by the Lateran Council of 1139 (Canon 7). Pope Alexander reaffirmed the law of clerical celibacy in 1180, as did the Council of Trent in the sixteenth century. There are two theories about its origin: one theory says that the law is divine law and cannot be overruled by the Church; the other says that it is Church law and so may, in principle, be changed.

The Roman Catholic Church has taken over from Judaism the doctrine that a priest must be unblemished. Thus eunuchs may not become priests, nor may deformed or illegitimate men. Here, as elsewhere, dispensation is possible, and is usual in the case of minor physical imperfections. The strong social reasons for forbidding illegitimate men to be priests counts against dispensation for them, however. If bastards could be priests the rule of celibacy might lead to a scandalous 'lineage' of illegitimate priests. All the same, in former times the Church probably had rather a struggle to ensure that only the legitimate entered the priesthood, as can be seen from the fact that emperors and other powerful persons were in the habit of placing illegitimate sons in good jobs in the Church as bishops, abbots and so on. Popes too sometimes found positions for their sons (disguised as nephews) in the family firm.

ISLAM

Muslim law is founded on the principle that God is the only law giver. It stems from the Koran, which is said to be God's word as transmitted to the prophet Mahomet, and is amplified on the one hand by the teachings and interpretations of judges, caliphs, imans and wise men, and on the other hand by the customs of people conquered or converted by Islam. These customs include those of the pre-Islamic Arabs themselves.

The Koran contains about 600 verses, most of which are concerned with prayer and ritual or are general exhortations about the truth of Islam and the goodness of God and the fates of believers and unbelievers in the afterlife. About 80 verses give ethical rules or laws and of those most have to do with marriage, divorce and the position of women. There are also important verses about the treatment of orphans, about adoption, and about inheritance. For some crimes (for example, adultery) there are punishments laid down; for others (for instance, wine drinking) no punishment is mentioned in the Koran itself, though early traditions authorize various sanctions such as flogging, death, amputation, and so on for transgressions such as wine drinking, homicide and theft. N. J. Coulson argues that the relative importance of marriage rules, divorce rules and inheritance law in the Koran and in early post-Koranic teaching reflects the change in Arab lands from tribal societies to societies based on the family.[25]

The enormous and rapid spread of Islam in the first centuries after the birth of Mahomet means that this religion has been deeply influenced by a large variety of local customs in the middle east, the far east, India and Africa. Thus the way in which the Koran is interpreted in Arab lands, for example, is still to some extent influenced by pre-Islamic Arab customs: the status of women in particular is so affected. Islam has many sects and for this and other reasons the legal systems of modern Muslim nations differ from each other as well as from the systems of non-Muslim lands. It is not possible therefore to generalize about Islamic law, but on the other hand there are certain basic beliefs shared by all Muslims and certain rules which, interpreted this way or that, can be seen in most or many Muslim nations.[26]

Marriage is enjoined on every Muslim and celibacy is condemned. The Prophet is reported as having once said 'An unmarried man is a brother of the devil'. Muslims may marry four wives, who must be monotheists. Marriage is regarded as a civil contract; its validity does not depend on a religious ceremony. There must be a dowry but its non-payment does not of itself invalidate a marriage. A girl can be married in infancy but can ratify or dissolve the contract on reaching puberty. Post-pubertal girls must consent to their marriage. The rules for what counts as consent differ according to whether the woman is a virgin or not: a virgin's consent is given by silence, by laughter or by tears; a non-virgin's consent – e.g., a widow's – must be given in words. A man's capacity to marry depends on the same factors that determine his capacity to make any valid contract – that is, he must have reached puberty and must understand what he is doing. The character of the contract differs between Sunni and Shia law. Sunni law says that the contract is invalid unless the girl's guardian consents to it; Shia law allows a girl to marry without the consent of her guardian.

The ceremony of marriage is not religious in character, as we have noted, and varies according to local custom. The bridegroom must formally consent to the marriage, and he is supposed to recite certain short verses from the Koran. The bride's consent is given through her attorney or guardian. She need not herself speak and in some places need not even be present. Muslims are enjoined to observe the civil law of the countries of their domicile: thus a Muslim domiciled in Britain would not be encouraged by his religious leaders to set up a polygamous family. (This does not mean that Muslims are not allowed to press for changes in the civil law of their countries of domicile.)

There are nine probibitions on marriage. A man cannot marry:

1. blood relations (e.g., his sisters, his nieces, his mother, etc.);
2. affinal relations (e.g., his daughter-in-law, his mother-in-law);
3. his foster mother (i.e., his wet-nurse) or his foster sister;
4. his wife's sister unless she is a divorcée;
5. a woman in *iddah* (the compulsory abstinence after divorce or widowhood which is required to establish the paternity of a possible child);
6. a polytheist;

7. his own slave;
8. his own divorced wife unless she has been married to another man in the interim;
9. a woman pregnant by another man.

In addition to these prohibitions, a Muslim woman is forbidden to marry any non-Muslim, whether polytheist or monotheist. Some sects forbid marriage during pilgrimage to Mecca.

Divorce (*talaq*) covers both divorce and nullity: rules for divorce occupy a very large percentage of space in Muslim legal writings. The rules are founded on the Koran,[27] amplified by the 'sayings of Mahomet'. Certain states of affairs positively require divorce. These are refusal to embrace Islam, apostasy, four months' celibacy after a vow and invalid marriage. Otherwise a woman needs a cause for divorce, but a man does not. (One of the 'sayings of Mahomet' is, 'A woman who asks for a divorce without a cause is forbidden to enter Paradise.') Causes which allow a woman to divorce her husband are the absence of (his) sexual organs, leprosy, impotence and evident madness. A man can divorce his wife in her presence, or in her absence, or through an agent by repeating the correct form of words the correct number of times; the details vary between different sects. A (Sunni) 'saying of Mahomet' is 'Every divorce is lawful except a madman's.' Thus in Sunni law future divorce ('I divorce you as from next week'), irregular divorce lacking the proper form of words and divorces made by drunken, drugged or dying men, although in some cases technically illegal, are nevertheless valid. Shia law, on the other hand, requires both that a man should fully intend to make a divorce and that the proper form of words should be used, before a divorce can be valid.

As well as four wives, a Muslim is allowed concubines; traditionally any slave woman can be made a concubine, the general idea being that concubines are those captured in war or purchased with money.[28]

In pre-Islamic Arab tribes only males inherited, but Koranic teaching is that females as well as males inherit. The principle is that different relatives, both male and female, are entitled to specific fractions of an estate. This can lead to difficulties and complications since in a large family the sum of the fractions is likely to exceed unity.

In Muslim law an illegitimate child has no (legal) father; he can, however, inherit from his mother. Since concubinage is legal the children of concubines are not illegitimate; in Africa, especially, the children of concubines have rights of inheritance similar to those held by children of wives, even though concubines themselves do not have the same rights as wives. In fact, a concubine may be best defined as a woman whose children have rights in a family though she herself does not: this definition marks off concubines from wives on the one hand, and whores on the other.

Illegitimate children are born of *zina* (forbidden sexual connection). Zina refers mainly to adultery and incest. The Koranic punishment for an adulterous wife is immuring.[29] Other traditional punishments include stoning (borrowed from Jewish law), decapitation, flogging, drowning and banishment. The seriousness of female adultery is shown by the fact that in some places it was customary for the guilty woman to be drowned by her own kinsfolk before she could be tried. In a proper trial proof was required, consisting in statements from four eye-witnesses (male) or a confession repeated four times.[30]

From time to time one can hear people deploring the common man's equation of morals and morality with sexual morality. It is fashionable among moral philosophers to assert that sexual morality is only a small part of morality *per se*. But this viewpoint ignores the historical fact that the major religions have always shown an extremely lively interest in all questions of sexual morality, so that teachings on sexual matters actually form a very large proportion of moral teaching *per se*. The interest is by no means dead, nor even slackening: for every Roman Catholic sermon preached against bank robbery there must be several thousand preached against contraception.

Why is this? Should we attribute it to the rise of capitalism? The phenomenon is too ancient and too widespread. Is it caused by the kinkiness of the celibate clergy? The phenomenon is not confined to them. Is the explanation Freudian, relating to the 'dark, irrational forces' which allegedly dominate all mankind? The reason, whatever it is, is certainly very ancient. The Bible vigorously condemns fornication, whoredom and adultery over and over again. It also condemns lying, homicide and idolatry. It is nowhere stated that the sins of sexuality are worse than other sins: nevertheless, the impression given is that they *are* because the Prophets in particular make sexual sins stand as symbols for other kinds of wickedness, and even for wickedness as such. Idolatry, lying and murder generally stand for idolatry, lying and murder in the Bible, but fornication, whoredom and adultery do not stand merely for impurity, incest, prostitution and marital infidelity; they are also common biblical metaphors for all the other sinful behaviour of mankind.

There is often a certain aptness in these metaphors. Thus when Jeremiah says:

> Oh . . . that I might leave my people, and go from them! for they be all adulterers, an assembly of treacherous men. . . .[31]

we are reminded that unless an adulterer happens to be a powerful tyrant who can do what he likes, he is bound to tell some lies – to his own wife, to his lover's husband, to the community in general. Otherwise his activities will be hampered by complaints or stopped by force. If adulterers have to tell lies, they are good symbols for liars. Ezekiel says that Jerusalem

> committed whoredoms in Egypt . . . doted upon the Assyrians her neighbours, captains and rulers clothed most gorgeously, horsemen riding upon horses, all of them desirable young men . . . increased her whoredoms . . . and doted upon [the Chaldeans]. . . . the Babylonians came to her into the bed of love, and they defiled her with their whoredom. . . .[32]

thus making whoredom and fornication a symbol of an incorrect foreign policy – not inaptly, really, for one kind of bad foreign policy involves selling one's country (the 'body' of the nation). Isaiah speaks of adultery meaning idolatry:

> But draw near hither, ye sons of the sorceress, the seed of the adulterer and the whore. . . . are ye not children of transgression, a seed of falsehood, enflaming yourselves with idols under every green tree, slaying the children in the valleys under the clifts of the rocks?[33]

The connection between the ideas of adultery and idolatry, it seems to me, is homicide. The lawful destruction of the adulterous man and woman – or of their infant, or their conceptus – has a mirror image in the unlawful human sacrifice demanded by religions which worship idols.

In Revelation, of course, whoredom is the be-all and end-all of wickedness:

> Babylon the great, the mother of harlots and abominations of the earth.[34]

One would not want to say that the appeal of the metaphor is due to its aptness only – there must be more to it than that. The idea that sexual sin is all sin must have some deep attraction for the human race. That is not to say, of course, that it is a true idea, but there may be some truth in it.

The common man's rough and ready equation between morals and sexual morals has some justification. Moral law *per se* substitutes right for might, regulating the relationships between the weak and the strong by reference to the former rather than the latter. Mankind's earliest perception of the dichotomies between weak versus strong and right versus might must have been its consciousness of male and female and of adult and child, so it is not surprising that the relationships between male and female and between adult and child turn out to be a basic concern, almost a defining property, of human morality.

Rules, customs and laws which regulate sexual relationships are bound to create distinctions between children – i.e., between those who ought and those who ought not to have been born. Whether it is mainly the children or mainly the parents who suffer the penalties imposed for forbidden intercourse or forbidden reproduction depends on the particular legal and moral system, and so too, of course, does the severity of the penalty. The questions of who shall suffer and how badly are not issues about which humanity or its lawgivers and prelates make a prior, conscious decision. Rather, the penalties grow out of the systematic distinction: they are then appealed to, both as reasons for preserving the *status quo* and as reasons for abolishing it. When the penalties fall mainly or entirely on one sex and not the other, or when they fall mainly on the child, then sooner or later there will be a cry for their abolition, because from inside the system the only really visible constituents of the legitimate/illegitimate distinction are the associated penalties.

CHAPTER 11

The Abolition of Illegitimacy

In 1978 Mr James White, MP, presented to the House of Commons 'A Bill to remove the legal disabilities of children born out of wedlock'. There are ten short paragraphs, of which the first reads:

> Not withstanding anything to the contrary, whether contained in any statutory order or rule of law, a child born out of wedlock shall have and enjoy rights, privileges and duties identical in all respects to those of other children.

The Bill was not passed. Abolishing the status of illegitimacy entails abolishing the distinction between legitimate and illegitimate birth, which in turn means abolishing or changing all the customary and legal arrangements for the maintenance of children. This may not be logically impossible, but it would require a thorough-going revision of private law – i.e., of the laws relating to maintenance, support, custody and guardianship, and testate and intestate succession. Radical revisions of this kind are likely to occur only at times of revolution: partial revision, on the other hand, being more gradual, has occurred in many countries during the last 150 years. Thus extensive revisions were attempted in France in 1794 and in Russia between 1917 and 1928, while in Britain, West Germany, New Zealand and the Nordic countries, for example, there has been quite a lot of piecemeal change.

THE FRENCH REVOLUTION AND THE LAW OF 12 BRUMAIRE[1]

The intention of the Law of 12 Brumaire (2 November 1793)

was to sweep away entirely all laws that differentiated between legitimate and illegitimate children. In 1794 the revolutionists declared, 'there are no bastards in France!' The old laws swept away by revolutionary reforms were, in summary, as follows.

A bastard could inherit from his mother, but from his father only if the father had no legitimate children. If there were no legitimate children, the bastard could inherit a maximum of one-sixth of the estate. The legitimate sons of a bastard could inherit from him: if he had none, his estate went to the state or to his *seigneur*. It was possible for a mother to take out filiation proceedings against the putative father, but only if he was unmarried. An unmarried putative father could be made to pay maintenance for the child if paternity could be proved. Proof of paternity consisted in establishing that there had been open cohabitation or that the father had admitted paternity in writing or in front of witnesses. If a woman had had sexual connection with more than one (unmarried) man, it was possible for her to claim against all of them for the payment of the lying-in expenses, and such claims were occasionally upheld by the courts. Legitimation by the king's grace was possible, and so too, of course, was legitimation by subsequent marriage, following canon law. Bastards born of adultery or incest could make no claim on either parent's estate. Illegitimate children were generally cared for in foundling homes run by religious orders.

Between 1790 and 1793 there was considerable discussion about the proposal to abolish the status of bastardy. On the one hand, it was argued that the distinction between legitimate and illegitimate people was founded on aristocratic, irrational, priestly notions. On the other hand, anxiety was expressed about inheritance. How can one have inheritance at all if no proof of paternity is required? What proof of paternity is reliable, apart from marriage? What would prevent prostitutes from fathering all their children on their richest customers? However, in spite of these doubts the Law of 12 Brumaire was adopted. Its provisions included the following.

Bastards were to have the same rights of inheritance against fathers as legitimate children. However, a bastard making a claim against an estate had to offer proof that he was indeed the son of the man whose estate it had been; proof had to consist in writings by the father or in evidence of a bastard son's having been maintained by him 'under the name of paternity' during his lifetime. The same requirements for proof of parentage were needed if a bastard made a claim against the estate of his mother. Subject to proof of parantage, bastards were to have the same rights of inheritance against collateral kin as those held by legitimate people. Bastards were to have a right to maintenance by their fathers if the father was unmarried, but a married father needed to pay only one-third of the sum that an unmarried man would have to pay.

The Law of 12 Brumaire was never really put into operation. In the first place, the courts usually ignored that part of it which dealt with inheritance, and, in the second place, the Commission of Civil Administration soon cancelled parts of the law by issuing directives. In 1795, for instance, the Commission sent out a brusque order: 'Legal actions concerning paternity are forbidden.' This meant that unmarried mothers were worse off than they had been under the old regime.

By the time the new Civil Code was finally agreed to and formulated great political changes had taken place. The Napoleonic Code dates from 1803 and does not reflect the original ideas of the revolutionists; with regard to bastardy, it was harsher than the laws of the ancient regime. Its provisions included the following.

The legitimation of children born of adultery or of incest was forbidden in all circumstances. The natural child, even if acknowledged by its father, could not have the same rights as the legitimate child. (This is explicitly stated in the Code.) Filiation proceedings against putative fathers, whether married or single, were forbidden in all circumstances, except when it could be proved of an unmarried man that he had forcibly abducted a single girl. Filiation proceedings against a mother were permitted unless the child was born of adultery or of incest. Certain rights of inheritance to limited amounts from the estate of a father were granted to bastards, but only to those born of single parents. Children of adultery and incest were explicitly excluded.

The differences between the Law of 12 Brumaire and the early Napoleonic Code can no doubt be explained mainly in terms of the political upheavals of the times. But it is also the case that the revolutionary demand to abolish the status of bastardy had never been widely agreed to. The anxieties expressed in the early years kept on reappearing. In 1798, for instance, D'Outrepont, a representative from Belgium, said in a speech to the Five Hundred:

> Natural Law does not recognize laws of inheritance. . . . the right to inherit is a social and civil institution; it is therefore clear that according to Natural Law the child born outside wedlock has no right to inherit from its father.[2]

Another speaker said:

> Paternity is Nature's secret, and Nature is silent. . . . it is also the mother's secret, but the mother's evidence is interested.[3]

A third representative urged that the father rather than the child needed protection:

> Marriage protects morals, and it is therefore essential that slander should not pursue the husband into the arms of his wife, that it should not strike in advance the young man in the heart of his betrothed.[4]

The revolutionists of 1789 did not appear to understand fully at first that in France at any rate legitimacy, illegitimacy and marriage are institutionally interdependent. They seemed to think that they could abolish the status of bastardy while retaining the marriage institution. Changes in the law governing the treatment of bastards were certain to have an effect on marriage and on property arrangements, and as soon as the revolutionists realized this, they opted to preserve and strengthen marriage, the family and property. After all, the institutions threatened were those of the bourgeoisie rather than those of the aristocracy.

The Napoleonic Code was just as harsh as England's New Poor Law of 1834. It was not until the Third Republic that any attempt was made to mitigate its harshness. The Code was condemned by many Frenchmen, including the radical Victor Hugo. In 1896 a new law granted certain additional rights of inheritance to bastards, and in 1912 the married man's immunity from filiation proceedings was removed, to the annoyance, no doubt, of many *pères de famille*.

RUSSIA AND THE BOLSHEVIKS[5]

In 1917, immediately after the October Revolution, the new rulers of Russia issued two decrees about marriage and divorce. One decree abolished religious marriage and instituted the civil registration of marriage; the other introduced the possibility of divorce by mutual consent.

In 1918 the Bolsheviks drew up their Code of Laws Relating to Acts of Civil Status, Marriage, Family and Guardianship. This Code stated, *inter alia*: 'Birth itself shall be the basis of the family. No differentiation whatsoever shall be made between relationship by birth in or out of wedlock.' This view of the family and of legitimacy was sustained, at least in theory, until 1944.

The abolition of the legal differentiation between children born in and out of wedlock was, in fact, to be achieved through three separate but roughly simultaneous sets of reforms, namely, changes in marriage law, changes in the law relating to wills and inheritance and changes in the law with respect to the rights and duties of caring for and supporting children.

Changes in marriage law

The Russian lawyer Vladimir Gsovski considers that the Soviet law on marriage laid down in the Civil Code of 1922 and 1926 is unique, having no parallel in, or similarity with, the marriage law of any other modern system. This view is based on the fact that the Code regards the civil registration of marriage, the only legally recognized formality of marriage, not as creating the state of wedlock but merely as providing evidence of its existence. Under the Code marriage itself is constituted by common household, cohabitation, mutual financial support and the raising of children together. It is marriage in this sense that is supposed to determine the disposition of marital property, the rights and succession of spouses and of children, and so on. Religious ceremonies cannot in law bring about marriage and are not taken as proof as its existence. Civil registration, although it does not create the state of marriage, is taken as proof of its existence.

The 1926 version of the Code expressly states that registration must be refused if one or both of the parties are under marriageable age (18 in most republics), of if they are full or half-brother and sister, or related in the direct line of descent or weak-minded or insane. It also states that registration is to be refused if either party is still bound by a registered or unregistered marriage. Apart from these restrictions on registration, the code is silent on adultery, bigamy and homosexuality, and it does not make incest a criminal offence. But some republics continued to treat incest as a criminal offence. That the 1926 Code gave tacit recognition to the legality of bigamy became apparent in 1929, when the Soviet Supreme Court allowed both the *de facto* wives of a dead man to share in the inheritance of his estate, on the grounds that each woman had been living with him before his death.

In the 1920s the Soviet Communist Party was very hostile towards the traditional Russian version of the family. Bukharin, addressing the Thirteenth Congress of the Communist Party of the Soviet Union in 1924, said: 'The family is a formidable stronghold of all the turpitudes of the old regime.'[6] The Soviet state too, was theoretically hostile towards the family, but it was beginning to discover that it is not easy to do without this institution.

Changes in the law relating to wills and inheritance

On 22 April 1918 the new government of Russia issued a decree about inheritance which said: 'Testate and intestate succession are hereby abolished. All the property of an owner becomes after his death the domain of the Russian Socialist Federal Soviet Republic.' Since the right to inherit is one of the main differences between legitimate and illegitimate children, the total abolition of this right must remove at least one distinction between the two. But the 1918 decree was qualified in two ways. First, in Tsarist Russia the law governing succession did not apply to freed serfs, who could not make wills. Hence among the peasantry succession was determined by local customs, not by law. Generally, a dead man's farm went to those relatives, male and female, who were living and working on it at the time of his death. The new Bolshevik decree was interpreted as applying only to those whose succession was already subject to the original Tsarist limitations. Second, in the small print of the decree itself it was stated that, until a scheme for universal social insurance had been set up, close relatives would be allowed to inherit property up to 10,000 gold roubles in value. The takeover by the state of insurance and social welfare took some time, and the Civil Code of 1922 therefore specifically allowed testate and intestate succession, retaining the upper limit of 10,000 roubles. The Code also set limits on the circle of people to whom property could descend: a testator could choose between his direct descendants, natural or adopted, born in or out of registered or unregistered wedlock; his spouse; and his disabled or property-less actual dependants. Intestate succession was similarly divided between descendants, spouse and dependants. In 1926 the upper limit of 10,000 roubles was removed. In 1928 a clause was added to the Code which made it illegal to disinherit a child of under 18 years of age. Three new classes of possible beneficiaries were added: the state, the Communist Party of the Soviet Union and certain professional organizations. In 1929 a 90 per cent death duty was introduced.

Changes in the law relating to child maintenance

In 1918 the Code of Laws Relating to Acts of Civil Status, Marriage, Family and Guardianship was drawn up. It stated that children and parents have no unconditional rights and duties of support. The duty of maintaining children falls on parents only if the children are not provided for by the state or from public funds, and children have a duty to support their aged parents only if the parents are not receiving old-age pensions or other kinds of social security payment. The principle that duties of maintenance do not arise unconditionally from family relationships is also to be seen in the 1926 Code, which states that a duty to maintain a spouse is conditional on a finding by a court that she or he is unable to work and is destitute, and that the obligated spouse is, in fact, able to render support. After a divorce any such obligation to support expires after a maximum period of 12 months.

According to the 1926 Code, the parent–child relationship is totally independent of marriage. Paternity, if established by a court, entails some liability to support a child and gives the child the right of succession. The 1918 qualification of the liability to support (which rendered support mandatory only in so far as the child was not supported by public or state funds) was quietly dropped. The task of providing for all children out of state funds had proved too great. Furthermore, the duty of support was extended, in the 1926 Code, to kin other than parents and to adoptive and foster parents. In cases in which a mother was not living with a man it became the duty of the court to discover the identity of the man or men with whom she had had sexual connection at the presumed time of conception, and to impose on one of them the duty to help maintain the child.

During the 1920s and 1930s there were many vagrant children in Russia. Some commentators have been tempted to explain this phenomenon by supposing that it was caused by a breakdown in marriage, the abolition of religion and the deliberate destruction of legal ties within the family. But there was juvenile vagrancy in Russia in Tsarist times too; and even in countries where the marriage bond has been solid and religious belief almost universal there has in the past been a great deal of childhood destitution – England in the nineteenth century is an example. A more probable explanation has to do with the fact that the 1920s, 1930s and 1940s were decades of major upheaval in Russia. The Revolution itself was followed by civil war; then came enforced collectivization and the mass transportation of peasants to Siberia, the Stalinist purges and the Second World War.

The vagrant children presented a problem which Stalin attempted to solve by a return to older ways. In 1935 a new law made parents liable to fines if their children committed acts of hooliganism or vandalism. Parents were also made jointly liable (with the children) for destructive actions committed by minors over the age of 14 whenever damages were payable. Minors over the age of 12 (lowered from 16) could be tried in the criminal courts (in 1941 the age was raised again, this time to 14). In 1943 Stalin established a number of reformatory colonies for the confinement, without judicial procedure, of minors aged between 11 and 16 who were wayward or vagrants or petty criminals. In 1944, in the middle of the war, he inaugurated the large-scale reform of Soviet marriage and divorce laws and of the laws concerning maintenance and support of children. In 1945 the law on inheritance was also reformed.

Since 1944 only a registered marriage has had the legal effect of marriage, creating rights and duties of husband and wife and of parenthood. The mother of a child born outside marriage can claim maintenance for the child from the father only if the child was born before 8 July 1944 and only if the father was registered as such in a civil Registry Office. Children born outside wedlock later than that date have no right of succession and may not use their father's name. The father has no duty to help support such children. Stalin, like Napoleon, abolished the paternity suit. However, in the Soviet Union all mothers receive aid from the state for the support of pre-school children; also, it is state policy to provide nurseries and crèches and to encourage mothers to seek employment outside their homes.

It is plain that the Bolshevik attempt to abolish the distinction between legitimate and illegitimate children did not last very long.

After 1928 testate succession remained limited to direct descendants, spouses and actual dependants. In 1945 it was widened to include brothers, sisters and parents, but narrowed to exclude children born out of registered wedlock. Testate and intestate succession follows a rule not unlike that of the Napoleonic Code. Three classes of beneficiaries are defined. Those in the third class can only succeed if there is no one in the first or second class; those in the second class inherit only if there is no first-class beneficiary. A child born outside wedlock can inherit if all three classes are empty. The three classes are: direct descendants born in wedlock, spouses and actual dependants; parents; brothers and sisters. There is a clause forbidding the disinheriting of minor children born in wedlock.

Since 1944 Soviet law has permitted the legitimation of children by subsequent marriage.

In 1947 Stalin, following a very old tradition, bought in a law which made marriage between Soviet nationals and foreigners illegal.

REFORM IN BRITAIN

Reform in Britain has come about largely as the result of the activities of pressure groups, the most important of which has been the National Council for the Unmarried Mother and her Child (NCUMC), now renamed the National Council for One-Parent Families (NCOPF).

The NCUMC came into being at a conference held in London on 14 February 1918. Its founder chairman was Lettice Fisher, a history don at Oxford married to another historian, H. A. L. Fisher. Her published works include books and papers on various social matters affecting women.[7]

Lettice Fisher was chairman of the NCUMC from 1918 until 1949. Virtually all the changes in the legal and social status of the illegitimate child in Britain which occurred during those years can be traced to the work and influence of the organization. When the NCUMC did not itself initiate legislative reforms it was at any rate consulted about them, often at its own insistence.

The events which led up to the creation of this organization were as follows. In 1914, the Child Welfare Council of social Welfare Associations, a body representing 70 associations concerned with the welfare of children, set up an enquiry office in London. The office was immediately overwhelmed with enquiries made by social workers on behalf of illegitimate children and by direct appeals for help from unmarried mothers. It thus became apparent that there was an urgent need for an organization to deal specifically with the welfare of illegitimate children and their mothers. The Council set up a special committee to look into the question and to decide upon the functions and policy of the proposed organization. While this committee was deliberating, the Registrar-General's report for 1916 was published.[8] It revealed that the mortality rate of illegitimate children was rising, while that of children in general was falling; expressed as a percentage of the infant mortality rate of legitimate children, the rate for illegitimates was 170 per cent in 1907 and 201 per cent in 1916. The total number of illegitimate births was also rising, from a pre-war figure of about 37,000 per annum to 41,000 in 1916. It rose again, to 44,000, in 1922.[9]

The special committee decided that the proposed new organization should have three functions: to obtain reform of the Bastardy Acts and of the Affiliation Acts; to secure the provision of adequate maternity care for unmarried mothers and adequate accommodation for unmarried mothers and their babies, with the special aim of allowing mother and baby to remain together wherever possible; to deal with individual enquiries and appeals for help.

In her monograph *21 Years and After* Lettice Fisher describes the difficulties encountered by the Council from the very beginning of its existence:

> Measures for the benefit of the unmarried mother were honestly regarded as a challenge to the accepted standards of morality, and the difficulty of getting workers, and indeed subscribers, to adopt a constructive rather than a deterrent policy, was considerable. . . . Unwearedly we explained that the child, whatever the faults and follies of its parents, was not to blame, and that the best method of helping it was to help its mother both before and after its birth.[10]

Because of hostility to its aims, the NCUMC suffered from a chronic shortage of money. In 1920, less than two years after its foundation, it nearly collapsed through lack of finance. It was rescued by a grant from another new organization, the National Council for Maternity and Child Welfare. The NCUMC and its successor, the NCOPF, has never been a popular charity. It was and still is seen by some as a threat to the stability of marriage, while others regard it as a vaguely ridiculous, possibly kill-joy enterprise run by earnest upper-middle-class ladies who devote their spare time to admonishing jolly girls and virile men.

The work of the NCUMC was from the first carried out by three major committees; the legal committee, the committee on homes and hostels and the care committee.

The legal committee drafted parliamentary Bills to be sponsored by the Council through its supporters in the House of Commons, and it considered and commented on all Bills connected with legitimation, affiliation, adoption, maternity care and so on. The first Bill sponsored by the Council itself was introduced in the House of Commons by Mr Neville Chamberlain in 1920. It is interesting to look at the proposals which, as it happens, the politicians of 1920 threw out as impractical and Utopian. Chamberlain's Bill provided for the legitimation of children by subsequent marriage, an increase in the *maximum* affiliation payment from 10 shillings (50p) a week to 40 shillings (£2) a week, and the appointment of officers to collect such payments. Although this Bill was thrown out, in 1926 the Government itself bought in a Legitimation Bill, so that Chamberlain's first provision did become law.

In 1926 the Government brought in its Adoption of Children Act. The NCUMC had given evidence to the parliamentary committees which drew up this Bill, for although it regarded adoption as a deplorable necessity, it believed that what adoption there was ought to be controlled by legal process.

In 1929 Neville Chamberlain was in charge of the huge Local Government Act which became law that year. Among its provisions was one which empowered local authorities to provide maternity care for pregnant women – and there was no proviso that the women must be married.

The NCUMC and the NCOPF, by drafting Bills, by giving evidence to parliamentary committees and to Royal Commissions and by suggesting amendments to proposed legislation has had, and continues to have, a considerable influence on British law making. No doubt its sister organizations in other countries exercise a somewhat similar influence on legislative bodies. Recently the NCOPF gave evidence before the Finer Commission, and several of its recommendations are incorporated in the Finer Report. Some of these have become law.[11]

In 1973 the National Council for the Unmarried Mother and her Child changed its name to the National Council for One-Parent Families.[12] It was felt that the illegitimate child (and its mother) could best be helped by stressing the similarities between its situation and needs and those of the children of widowers, widows and divorced people. One of the main present aims of the NCOPF is to try to make sure that laws intended to help children do not exclude the illegitimate child, either on purpose or by accident.

NORWAY'S CASTBERG LAWS

The official Protestant ethic of the lands of northern Europe in the nineteenth century was not especially tolerant of sexual misdemeanours, but, like the early Puritans of England and America, Scandinavian Protestants adopted a punitive attitude towards the fathers as well as the mothers of illegitimate children. This has not necessarily made society any less critical, but it has affected maintenance. For the last 200 years the overall tendency of the relevant legislation in Norway, as in the rest of Scandinavia, has been to make the father pay as well as the mother. Maintenance rights of illegitimate children over both parents have been gradually increased, and so have inheritance rights, first in respect of the mother and mother's kin, more recently in respect of the father and father's kin.

Modern Norwegian legislation concerned with illegitimacy is founded on the 1915 Castberg Laws,[13] named after the politician Johann Castberg. Modern Swedish legislation on legitimacy and illegitimacy also dates from 1915. Finland introduced a similar set of laws in 1922, and Denmark in 1923.

Under the Castberg Laws a distinction was made between *legal paternity* and *possible paternity*, each status carrying certain initial legal obligations. Any man who was known to have had sexual connection with the mother of an illegitimate child at the presumed time of conception counted as a possible father and had an initial legal obligation to maintain the child; if more than one man was involved, each one was technically liable for the whole sum of maintenance payable. Under the original version of the Castberg Laws, a mother who claimed maintenance from more than one man could be placed under legal guardianship; normally the mother had custody of an illegitimate child, but a mother under guardianship could lose custody of the child, since custody was not granted to the mother if this was judged contrary to the best interests of the child. The legal obligation of the possible father or fathers to pay maintenance means that the mother's promiscuity cannot deprive the child of a legal right to be supported by members of its community.

In Norway the local authorities have a legal duty to initiate legal proceedings against putative fathers if no one admits paternity. It is quite usual, however, for a man to admit paternity. In 1960 about one-third of the putative fathers sued contested the claim. Of these, one-fifth were exonerated. Legal paternity is established by one man's admitting paternity, or by biological tests and proofs, or by other evidence. Proof of legal paternity requires stronger evidence than proof of possible paternity. If legal paternity is established, it entails rights of inheritance as well as rights of maintenance, and it cancels the obligations of any other men who have had sexual relations with the mother.

The mother, as well as the father, has a legal duty to help maintain an illegitimate child; the child is supposed to be brought up at the standard of living of the richer parent.

If a man admits paternity, he is given an opportunity to make maintenance payments voluntarily, though, naturally, it is not up to him alone to decide how much or how little. If he admits paternity but refuses to pay maintenance, or if he is judged to be the legal father and refuses to pay, a writ can be issued against him. But since 1915 a climate of opinion has grown up in Norway (and, indeed, in all the Scandinavian countries) in which it is more or less taken for granted that if a man believes himself to be, in all probability, the father of an illegitimate child, he will make a financial contribution towards its upkeep, sharing the burden with the mother, without having to be dragged through the courts first.

Johann Castberg was asked by journalists and others whether he did not think that the Castberg Laws might endanger the institution of marriage in Norway. He replied that, in his view, the institution of marriage fulfilled a basic human need for love, security and stability and could not be endangered by purely economic reforms.[14]

Unmarried fathers, like divorced fathers, sometimes pay up voluntarily for the support of their children but sometimes refuse. Refusal may be prompted by any number of different reasons, some of them subjective (such as dislike of the child or of the mother), some nasty (such as pure stinginess) and some comparatively reasonable. One of the more reasonable reasons for refusing is that the man has married or remarried and has acquired new obligations which might actually prevent him from fulfilling the old ones. Now, his ability to marry (or to remarry) is itself the inevitable consequence of the fact that he was unmarried (or divorced) in the first place. It would seem, then, that laws like the Castberg Laws cannot place the illegitimate child in *exactly* the same economic position as the legitimate child.

NEW ZEALAND'S REFORMS OF 1969

The Status of Children Act, 1969, was intended to abolish the status of illegitimacy in New Zealand. It says, *inter alia*:

> For all purposes of the law in New Zealand the relationship between every person and his father and mother shall be determined irrespective of whether the father and mother are or have been married to each other, and all relationships shall be determined accordingly.

Two other acts provide supporting legislation.

The Domestic Proceedings Act of 1968 states: 'The same support remedies are available to children born in wedlock and to children born out of wedlock.' A mother, or a child welfare officer with the mother's consent, or a grandparent, or a guardian, or any person acting with the approval of the court, may bring an action for maintenance against the father of a child which is not being properly supported by him. If the father has custody of the child, he may bring action against its mother for a contribution towards its support. These rules apply both to children born in wedlock and to those born out of wedlock, but in the latter case an order can be made against a man only if a paternity order has already been made against him, or if he has been declared to be the father by a court, or has admitted paternity in writing, or has been appointed the guardian of the child, or is stated to be the child's father on its birth certificate. The mother or the child through a guardian can apply for a declaration of paternity. A man can be registered as the father of a child whether or not he and its mother are married to each other, provided he gives his permission, or has lived as the *de facto* husband of the child's mother before its birth. Registration counts as *prima facie* evidence of paternity. Mothers, children and putative fathers can all be compelled to have blood tests if ordered to do so by a court.

The Guardianship Act of 1968 divides children born out of wedlock into two classes: those whose parents live, or have lived, as man and wife, and those not in that situation. In the second case the mother is the sole guardian of the child; in the former, the two parents are equal guardians. If a man has at any time been married to the mother of the child, or if he is the legal guardian of the child, his permission is needed before the child can be given for adoption. The mother's permission is also needed. A man is entitled to apply for sole or joint guardianship of a child which be believes to be his; cases are decided on their merits. A child born out of wedlock takes its mother's surname.

The laws of succession in New Zealand now allow a child born out of wedlock to inherit under its father's will and under an intestacy, provided the relationship is known. Such a child can also, in theory, inherit from collateral kin who die intestate. But the Status of Children Act does specifically absolve executors from the duty of tracing the offspring (other than those born in wedlock) of a dead man's brothers, sisters, uncles, etc.

New Zealand has a mixed economy and comparatively heavy taxation. It is a welfare state. There are maternity allowances, child allowances and some special allowances for single mothers.

SWEDEN IN 1980

According to the Swedish jurist Anders Agell, 'The formal pattern of family formation has changed more rapidly in Sweden than in most other parts of the world.'[15] This can be seen from the statistics relating to birth. In 1956 10.2 per cent of children in Sweden were born outside wedlock (a percentage not uncharacteristic of Europe as a whole); in 1966 the figure was 14.6 per cent, in 1971 21.7 per cent and in 1979 37.5 per cent. Most of the children born out of wedlock live with two parents. Between 5 and 6 per cent of unmarried mothers live alone; the rest cohabit with more or less permanent partners, either the fathers or, sometimes, the stepfathers of their children.

In medieval times in Sweden marriage law involved marriage contracts. These often involved financial settlements. After the contract had been drawn up and agreed to, there would be a wedding ceremony, with a so-called 'bedding'. Since the marriage took part in two stages, there could sometimes be uncertainty as to whether two people were married or not, and this led to the formation of the notion of incomplete marriage. The Swedish Civil Code of 1734 provided for the first time in law that certain legal effects arose as the result of incomplete marriages. Thus a woman could sue for a court ruling that she was indeed the wife of such-and-such a man if she had been betrothed to him (contracted to marry him) and had had intercourse with him but had not been through the religious ceremony. Most, though not all, marital law effects followed from the court ruling. One result of this was that a man could be declared married in his absence and against his will, and also prevented from marrying anyone else. On the other hand, it protected women who had betrothed themselves in all good faith to men who turned out to be philanderers.

The 1734 Code was repealed in 1915, and the institution of incomplete marriage disappeared from the statutes. The notion of incomplete marriage was replaced by that of breach of promise, and rules were set up under which a betrothed woman could sue the man for damages if he refused to marry her. In 1915 the terms 'legitimate' and 'illegitimate' were deleted from the texts of statutes and the terms 'born in/out of wedlock' substituted.

In 1973 all rules relating to betrothal were removed from Swedish marriage law; and in 1976 the terms 'born in/out of wedlock' were deleted from the statutes.

In 1969 the Swedish government issued a directive to the legislative committee on family law then deliberating on marriage, divorce, etc. The directive stated that marriage occupied, and ought to occupy, a central position within family law; nevertheless, an endeavour should be made to ensure that legislation did not contain any provisions which would create difficulties or inconvenience for people who had children and had formed families without marrying. It was further stated that legislation should be neutral in relation to different forms of cohabitation and different possible moral attitudes towards sexual unions. In the government Bill on family law passed in 1973 similar views were expressed by the Minister responsible, who said that it was important that people's freedom to frame their personal lives for themselves should be respected. According to the 1973 law on marriage, marriage law rules apply only to married people, yet at the same time, 'having regard to the custody of children and the right to a common dwelling, there should be uniform rules for all cohabitating couples.' In Swedish tax law and law on social benefit payments (as against marriage law *per se*) it is the case anyway that married and unmarried parents receive the same treatment. The marriage law, however, appears to contain contradictory ideas. It also seems to be the case that different areas of the law can pull in different directions. The legal situation of cohabitating men and women, whether married or not, is affected by marriage law, the law of contract (which determines, for example, who owns or has rights in the common dwelling), the Parents and Children Code, the tax laws and the laws on inheritance.

Marriage law incorporates rules about property. In Nordic countries the law is that each partner owns his or her property separately, both before and after marriage. However in the event of death, the spouse is the heir in law if there are no children; further, in the case of separation, some types of property held by the two parties become 'communal' and is divided equally between them. Cohabitating partners, unlike married partners, do not have a legal right to a share of communal property when they separate.

Cohabitating partners have no rights or duties in law to maintain each other either during or after the cohabitation period. The marriage law, on the other hand, does give a divorced woman the right to sue for alimony unless she has remarried or is cohabitating with another man.

Under the Parents and Children Code biological parents of both sexes have a duty to support their children and to pay maintenance in event of separation or divorce. Step-parents also have a legal duty to pay for support and maintenance, but the first duty in case of conflict is to one's biological children. The term 'step-child' includes the child of one's cohabitating partner, but only if the cohabitating couple also have a biological child of their own. Married couples are joint guardians of their children, but an unmarried mother is the sole guardian of her child and has sole custody, whether she is living with the father or not. However, if the father and mother of a child born out of wedlock apply to the court, they may be given joint custody. Disputes about the custody of a child are, if taken to court, settled by reference to 'the best interests of the child', irrespective of whether the parents are married, unmarried or divorced. For a father to be given custody of a child, he must have lived with it in the same dwelling, which means in effect that he must have cohabited with its mother, married or unmarried as the case may be.

According to the Names Act of 1963, a wife takes her husband's surname but has the right to keep her own name if she wishes. Normally a child takes its mother's surname, which, if she is married, is usually also her husband's surname. However, a child born out of wedlock can be given its father's surname if the parent who has custody so wishes. The parent must then notify the civil registration authority to that effect.

Marriage legislation in Sweden and the other Nordic countries is secular. It consists of a set of practical rules on maintenance, property, wills and succession. Several of the rules are protective – i.e., they protect one or other party, and also the children of the marriage, against the consequences of death, divorce and disputes of various kinds. Children, in particular, are protected by being given certain rights to support and certain rights of inheritance. Marriage codes which are non-secular – e.g., the marriage law of Israel – also, of course, contain practical rules on maintenance, property and inheritance but non-secular marriage law does not consist entirely of such practical rules and prescriptions, as was noted in chapter 10. Secular marriage law, combined with easy divorce arrangements, means that marriage is rather like a revocable contract. That being so, there does not seem to be any strong reason why people should cohabit rather than marry or vice versa. On balance, it would seem to be in the interests of the parties, and also of the community as a whole, if all cohabitations were in fact legal marriages, since this would allow Sweden to have just one set of family law rules, which would then apply to nearly all children, very many sexual partnerships, nearly all inheritance and so on. As it is, in Sweden there are three overlapping sets of family law rules, one for married people and their children, one for unmarried cohabiting couples and their children and one for unmarried non-cohabiting couples and their children. There does not seem to be any particular point in having three sets of rules rather than one set, and the existence of three sets may involve just the kind of disadvantage for the child born out of wedlock that the Swedes are trying to abolish. On the other hand, if the differences between the sets of rules are slight, there does not seem much point in trying to smooth everything out merely for the sake of tidiness. Anders Agell writes:

> If legislation continues as at present [in Sweden] this will mean the construction for cohabitation between men and women of a system of rules which is an alternative to marriage. In Sweden . . . it should be sufficient to have only one legal institution, whether it be called marriage or something else . . . if the marriage rate remains low it will not be possible to maintain two sets of rules and instead there will be a change-over such that long-term cohabitation will become completely equivalent to marriage. . . . Why not then encourage the contracting of marriages? . . . The State as legislator ought to find it in its interest that long-term cohabiting couples should marry, so that they would be covered by the complete set of rules for marriage.[16]

Agell does not say what should be done about short-term cohabitations, nor has he any suggestions for rules to protect the child of short-term cohabitations.

If we look at the attempts to abolish the status of bastardy described in this chapter, we may notice two separate theories about how to do it. There is, first, the idea that the difference between legitimacy and illegitimacy can be done away with by making every biological father responsible for the maintenance of his child, whether or not he is married to its mother. However, for this idea to work there have to be rules for determining paternity; fathers cannot be made responsible in law for the upkeep of children unless it can be established who a child's father is. Marriage is, at present, the institution which enables everyone to know who a child's father is in the majority of cases. It is also the institution which, paradigmatically, generates the distinction between legitimacy and illegitimacy. If marriage is abolished or becomes a minority cult, new rules for the determining of paternity will have to be invented. The difficulty, of course, is to invent a set of rules for determining paternity which will not automatically generate a new distinction analogous to the present distinction between legitimacy and illegitimacy.

This problem, together with the fact that marriage law and property law are always connected, has led people to the second, left-wing theory. In its extreme form, that favoured by the early Bolsheviks and by various modern radicals and by the Chinese state (as far as one can judge), this theory claims that the care of *all* children should be the direct responsibility of the state. The idea goes along with an attack on 'the family'. Bukharin, as we have seen, said that 'the family' was the locus of ancient turpitudes. Wilhelm Reich, a radical psychoanalytic writer, described 'the family' as *the vassal factory*. (And what is a state kindergarten?) Attacks like this on 'the family' ignore the fact that most real children prefer not to be raised in orphanages, foundling homes or boarding schools. Instead of introducing or reintroducing baby farms of one kind or another, it would be better to examine the different varieties of family possible. For there is no such thing as 'the' family, but rather several different ways of organizing sexual, social and economic relationships within kin groups.

In New Zealand, Norway, Sweden and several other modern states the responsibility for the support of a child born out of wedlock is shared between its mother, its father and the state itself. Changes in the status of women and enormous increases in taxation and welfare legislation mean that the legitimate child too is supported partly by its parents and partly by the state, for even the children of wealthy parents are eligible for free or subsidized health care, free or subsidized education and so on.

In modern states two sets of rules for determining paternity exist side by side. On the one hand, there is the traditional set of rules which make up the institution of marriage, and, on the other hand, there are rather complex sets of more or less ad hoc regulations covering things like filiation proceedings, declarations of paternity, blood tests, etc. Responsibility is entailed l parenthood, however established, but the state itself (suppl mented by certain charities) is a kind of safety-net and will, the last resort, completely support any child within its borde if no one else will.

CHAPTER 12

Illegitimacy and Illicit Birth

Most ideas are to some extent elastic and 'inexact'. Even supposedly exact ideas may allow of boderline cases, at the very least in the form of defective examples. Thus in ordinary life we often behave as if three straight lines which do not quite enclose a space still make a kind of triangle and as if a slightly flattened circle is nevertheless a sort of circle. On the other hand, it would be surprising if philosophers or others were to produce rival and incompatible definitions of these relatively simple mathematical ideas in the way that they do, in fact, produce rival and seemingly incompatible definitions of more difficult notions.

Wittgenstein argues that there are concepts which have no 'rigid limits': a non-rigid concept covers

> a complicated network of similarities, overlapping and criss-crossing: sometimes overall similarities, sometimes similarities of detail. . . . I can think of no better expression to characterize these similarities than 'family resemblances'.[1]

As examples of family resemblance concepts Wittgenstein gives number, game, language, goodness, knowledge, fear and understanding.

> Why do we call something a number? Well, perhaps because it has a – direct – relationship with several things that have hitherto been called number: and this can be said to give it an indirect relationship to other things we call the same name. And we extend our concept of number as in spinning a thread we twist fibre on fibre. And the strength of the thread does not reside in the fact that some one fibre runs through its whole length, but in the overlapping of many fibres.[2]

J. R. Bambrough goes so far as to imply that *all* concepts are family resemblance concepts – that is, that there is no such thing as a concept with a single 'fibre'.[3] But this is extremism.

G. E. M. Anscombe has suggested that some notions – she deals specifically with the notion of murder – are made up of cores and penumbrae.[4] Thus, for example, killing an innocent man deliberately and intentionally counts as a core case of murder, whereas killing a man by irresponsible firing into a crowd just for fun is a penumbral case. *Penumbra* is not the same thing as *borderline*; a case in the penumbra is a clear case of murder (or whatever), not a doubtful case. Cases in the penumbra might be said to have a 'direct' relationship with core cases in the way that new types of number (in Wittgenstein's example) have a direct relationship with old types; and penumbral cases have an 'indirect' relationship with each other in the way Wittgenstein describes new types of number having 'indirect' mutual relationships. So a concept consisting of core and penumbra could be regarded, possibly, as exemplifying a subspecies of family resemblance concepts.

The notion of illegitimacy can be regarded either as a special case of, or as co-extensive with, the idea of illicit birth. *Qua* special case, it is definable in a variety of different ways.

1. It can be defined as resulting from illicit intercourse, which illicit intercourse may or may not be punishable in law.
2. It can be defined as involving legal or customary exclusion from some social group (e.g., family, or lineage, or clan, or tribe, or race, or caste, or religious community, or some or all of these), and such exclusion may or may not entail loss of rights.
3. It can be defined precisely in terms of lack of rights: for example, lack or loss of property rights, lack or loss of a right to some job or social role such as the priesthood, the monarchy, etc.
4. It can be defined (though only partly) in terms of social stigma, contempt and scorn, low status, etc. Such things, even if not exactly *defining properties*, are certainly thought of as *criteria*, particularly by anthropologists.

Illicit birth, in turn, can be illicit for a variety of possible reasons. To begin with, it may be illicit either because it results from illicit intercourse or for some other reason. Illicit intercourse, again, may be illicit for a variety of possible reasons, depending on the society in question. Possible types of illicit intercourse include the following: intercourse in a marriage rendered void or invalid by reason of incest, illegal miscegnation, caste barriers or mixed religion; adulterous intercourse; simple incest without attempted marriage; premarital intercourse. Birth following permitted intercourse can also, in some circumstances, count as illicit, being forbidden or discouraged by law or custom, again for a variety of possible reasons: a child may be 'unwanted' (i.e., unlikely to be supported by its parents); there may be reasons associated with population control; intercourse may be permitted but specifically only for religious or 'fun' reasons (e.g., the orgies of the Areoi,[5] sex in brothels); eugenic factors may impose restrictions. There is plainly a lot of 'criss-crossing' here; further, several different possible core notions are apparently available.

The man in the street thinks of an illegitimate child simply as a baby born to an unmarried girl. This somewhat naive notion is shared by social workers and by cause-oriented sociologists; thus adulterine bastardy is generally excluded from the case books of social workers, and, less excusably, from the dissertations of certain sociologists.[6] Lawyers know, of course, that it is possible for a married woman to have an illegitimate child. An educated layman with some awareness of the legal system and of the existence of anthropology probably thinks of illegitimacy in terms of a core notion (*a child born out of wedlock*) supplemented by a penumbra (e.g. *a child born of detected adultery* – plus, perhaps, some foreign variants). Anthropologists (for instance, Malinowski), writing as if in search of an essence or 'single fibre' common to out-of-wedlock illegitimacy and adulterine bastardy, and professionally conscious, of course, of ethnographic variety, define legitimacy and illegitimacy in terms of the child's relationship to a recognized male guardian or sociological father. But since the ethnographic possibilities include legal systems which allow an illegitimate child to be legitimized through adoption by a female guardian, it is necessary to add to the new core notion of legitimacy (*a child with a recognized male guardian*) the penumbral case of *a child with a recognized female guardian*. Matrilineal polyandrous societies generate another penumbral possibility: *a child with one or more recognized male guardians*. By this time we may feel the need for a third definition: *(Il)legitimate child = a child conceived and born in circumstances which do/do not conform to the rules governing birth and conception in the parents' community* – a core which still needs a penumbra, however, in order to allow for the de-bastardizing processes (such as adoption) which are available in some legal systems.

This third definition, core and penumbra, seems to me to be reasonably adequate, though it must be admitted that the idea of illegitimacy has now come as close as may be to the idea of illicit birth and is no longer obviously a special case of that kind of birth. However, the rules which govern birth and conception may well happen to include rules which have nothing to do with family formation or marriage: this is a reason against equating illegitimacy with illicit birth.

ILLICIT INTERCOURSE

Incest seems to be a rather basic type of illicit intercourse, since it is banned virtually everywhere and is said to provoke unique feelings of horror in most societies. Unlike adultery which, under one description or another, is also forbidden in most societies, incest does not logically presuppose the idea of property; in particular, it does not presuppose the idea that women, or marriage partners, are possessions. Incest *per se* is not a kind of theft, whereas adultery is at least partly just that. The ban on incest has been compared with the – supposedly instinctive – avoidance of in-breeding seen in some wild animals: for example, it has been compared with the solitary hunting and roaming which young male lions engage in for several years before they mate and which effectively reduces the possibility of their mating with closely related females. The teleological point of this leonine behaviour seems to be to extend the gene pool by preventing incest, and it is only one example of animal mating behaviour which has that same point. Since incest is anyway biologically defined, it is not easy to imagine its being defined out of existence, whereas it does seem logically possible to define adultery out of existence, not by redefining it but by redefining marriage. Thus although a human society based on 'open marriage' may not be empirically possible, it is surely logically possible, and the logical possibility is one under which the term 'adultery' would cease to have any application. To imagine a society with no logical possibility of incest would involve imagining a biologically different species (e.g., a hermaphroditic species). For these reasons legalizing incest is not on a par with legalizing extramarital or adulterous sexual activity; defenders of the permissive society, however, treat the bans on incest, homosexuality, adultery and premarital sex as similarly based.

J. Goody has pointed out certain problems relating to the definition of incest.[7] On the one hand, the scope of the term is not clear – it does not have 'rigid limits'; on the other hand, the core notion which Europeans perhaps think of as atomic might seem to other societies not atomic but molecular, i.e., made up of a conglomeration of ideas rather than having a simple centre. Third, Goody says,

> the whole lengthy discussion of incest has turned on the supposition that it is a type of illicit sexual intercourse which is characterized by a particular horror. In the Western European system it is true that the entire range of offences included under the category incest is so regarded. But in many other societies, this is not so.[8]

The *Oxford English Dictionary* defines incest as 'sexual relation between near kindred' (here 'near kindred' presumably means members of the nuclear or elementary family). Other dictionaries give a wider definition. *Webster's*, for example, defines incest as 'sexual commerce between persons so related by marriage or affinity that legal marriage cannot take place between them'. In English law the 'persons so related' include half-brothers and half-sisters, step-parents and step-children, adopting parents and their adopted children. Various in-laws are or were once 'persons so related' (e.g., the deceased wife's sister). Under Muslim law, to take a foreign example, a man may not marry his foster mother (wet-nurse) or her daughters, for these persons are, as it were, symbolic blood relations and hence fall under the incest taboo.

We might think of the narrower definition in the *Oxford English Dictionary* as giving the core notion and the wider one in *Webster's* as adding a penumbra and some borderline cases or as covering cases which are penumbral in some societies and borderline in others. Goody, however, in effect raises the question of whether the core notion is a unitary notion which cannot be further divided:

> Both definitions [i.e., that of the *Oxford English Dictionary* and *Webster's*] are clearly based upon the institutions of our own society, where prohibitions on intercourse, like prohibitions on marriage, are bilaterally arranged (i.e., as between maternal and paternal relatives) within limited ranges of kin. But are they necessarily adequate for the analysis of non-European societies?[9]

He argues that these definitions are, in fact, inadequate on the grounds that the European system of classifying sexual offences is not universal and is, generally speaking, simpler (i.e., has fewer categories) than some African and Pacific Island classificatory schemes. Thus the (matrilineal) Ashanti distinguish terminologically between sexual intercourse with female members of the matriclan and sexual intercourse with female members of the patriclan: both types of intercourse are seriously criminal in Ashanti law (in fact, both are punishable by death) but, according to Goody, citing Rattray:

> The terminological distinction indicates that it is intercourse within the matriclan which is the major prohibition here while that within the patrilineal subgroup is subsidiary.[10]

The Ashanti word for the major crime has the meaning 'the eating up of one's own blood'. The Ashanti also distinguish between, on the one hand, adultery with the wives of members of the same descent group and, on the other hand, adultery with the wives of unrelated men; the former is regarded as much more serious than the latter. (More serious than either is adultery with a chief's wife.) Another African people, the Tallensi, who are patrilineal, have only one word to describe all types of (heterosexual) sexual offence, but Goody argues that they have an implicit threefold classification which, though not signposted by terminology, can be inferred from their system of customary punishments and which divides heterosexual offences into three main kinds: intercourse with members of the (inner) patriclan, intercourse with wives of members of the patriclan, and intercourse with wives of non-clansmen.

Goody concludes from these and other examples that an adequate cross-cultural analysis of illicit extramarital hetero-sexual intercourse requires a system of classification which is both more complex and more precise than that provided by the overlapping categories of adultery, incest and fornication. It follows that we cannot flatly state that incest is regarded as a crime in all human societies; but it does seem to be true all the same that, as far as is known, all human societies think of sexual commerce between close relatives (defined this way or that) as a type, or as types, of illicit intercourse. It has already been noted in earlier chapters that in European countries children known to have been born of incest have a specially low status even among bastards,[11] and that in some systems of traditional law the term 'bastard' itself refers primarily to children born either of incest or of adultery.[12]

Premarital intercourse is a less serious form of illicit inter-course: in certain circumstances it is not illicit at all. In the past in some European peasant communities intercourse between properly betrothed but not yet married couples was considered alright; in later and stricter times a publicly announced engagement could appease family anger generated by the dis-covery that a daughter had acquired a secret lover. In England permanent unions or *de facto* marriages have always had much the same legal consequences as genuine marriages, provided that neither party is married in law to someone else. Premarital intercourse which can be easily remedied – i.e., followed by a prompt wedding if pregnancy ensues – is obviously a less serious matter than intercourse between parties who, for one reason or another, are not able to marry. It seems probable therefore that, other things being equal, polygynous societies will not condemn premarital intercourse as much as mono-gamous societies do. The fact that, according to traditional Jewish law, the child of an unmarried girl is not necessarily a *manzer* is doubtless a long-range consequence of the fact that the Jews were once polygynous. When contraception and abortion are legal, reliable, safe and available, premarital intercourse may become the norm (as we can see from our own society today), thus proving that rules prescribing it are concerned with reproduction and not with purity. This is confirmed by the fact that the abolition of laws against fornication and bastardy does not by itself render these things licit in the eyes of the community. The last of such laws was removed from the English statute books in 1834, but the social distinction between good and respectable girls on the one hand and unrespectable girls ruined by sexual intercourse on the other became even stricter during the nineteenth and early twentieth centuries. It began to be eroded after the First World War but was still in force in a muted form until the invention of hormone-based contraceptives in the 1960s abolished it, as it were, overnight.

ILLICIT REPRODUCTION

Birth is not solely a private, 'family' matter; it is a matter in which the whole community has an interest. The interest shows itself in rules and regulations, laid down by religion and by the state, which tell individuals when and with whom they are permitted to mate and when and in what marital and financial circumstances they are permitted to multiply the race. In the past religion and the state have sought to control mating; today – partly because of the invention of reliable methods of contraception and partly for demographic reasons – the community seeks rather to control reproduction itself, in some countries through state-approved ideology and propaganda, in others via the direct use of state power, with or without the sanction of religion. A human community is a mutual-aid system, and it is always in a position to make things tough for non-conforming individuals by withdrawing or reducing normal aid: more extreme measures such as tax penalties, ostracism, physical violence, imprisonment, and death, are also at its disposal. Taking the world as a whole, it is apparent that all the above-mentioned means, from the mildest propaganda right up to the death penalty, have been used at one time or another, in once place or another, for the purpose of backing up rules which control and regulate mating and reproduction.

Does the state, does the community have any *right* to interfere in matters relating to reproduction? It seems to me that it must have rights in this area because it has duties, and a duty to do such-and-such implies a right to do such-and-such. Presumably, even the simplest human communities give shelter and sustenance and midwifery help to women in labour: the community has that duty and pregnant women have that right – how else could life go on? Children are supported not only by their families but also by social arrangements that provide education and hospitals and tax rebates, and social security payments and soup kitchens and, more generally, by community respect for the integrity of the elementary family – how else, in a sophisticated society, could life go on? But the duties of the community and of the state are not open-ended. It is anyway inevitable that limits will be drawn and that a distinction will be made between licit and illicit reproduction. This has always been the case, and the only question is whether the ways in which the limits and distinctions are drawn and enforced are consonant with human welfare and with justice and with a rational view of the duties of the state.

Marriage laws and inheritance laws provide a framework which enables human beings to produce and successfully rear the members of the next generation. If mating and reproduction were entirely random, and if communities took no interest whatsoever in family formation and child rearing, the existence of civilization, and possibly even that of the race, would be jeopardized. Thus the Christian Church – e.g., the Roman Catholic Church – is right, in a way, to describe marriage as a 'remedy for evil' because the problems or evils associated specifically with sex and reproduction are in fact dealt with, to some extent at least, by precisely this institution. On the other hand, the marriage institution *per se*, however perfect, is not apt for dealing with all the problems and evils connected with sex and reproduction. For example, marriage *per se* is not apt for dealing with the purely medical problems associated with childbirth (a fact which, in the main, the Church recognises); nor is it apt for dealing with the problem of overpopulation.

The Church, naturally enough, regards Christian teaching on marriage and related matters as more or less complete, needing no additions from Engels, Freud or Marie Stopes. Thus some Roman Catholic traditionalists are forced into the position of asserting that there is no such thing as overpopulation, that no demographic state of affairs could conceivably count as *too many*. At the other extreme are those panicky people who think that *all* our political, economic and ecological difficulties are caused by populations that are too large. It is surely possible to avoid both these extremes, to acknowledge, on the one hand, that there could well be such a thing as too many people and that marriage institutions *per se* cannot cure that particular evil, and to admit, on the other hand, that too many people is not the worst of all possible disasters and that some conceivable cures (war, compulsory sterilization, mass infanticide) would be worse than the disease.

Some marriage customs, in fact, do discourage overpopulation, more or less by accident. Thus a country with many celibate religious, and with no hostility to celibacy among lay people, and with a late average age of marriage may well have a stable population. This seems to be the case with Ireland. However, the traditions of Ireland hardly provide a general solution. For one thing, it is quite impossible to imagine Africans, Indians, Japanese and Chinese adopting Irish customs and becoming just like the folk in Dublin.

In much of Africa and Asia marriage is virtually universal. All adult individuals, but especially women, are expected to marry. Outside Buddhist monasteries the option of personally chosen celibacy is just not available. Arranged marriages are the norm in many African and Asian countries, and girls usually marry young, at about 15 or 16. Even in Westernized Japan an unmarried woman is a social anomaly and an embarrassment to her family.

India attempts to control the size of its population by vigorous birth-control campaigns and by sterilization campaigns; China also uses these means and, furthermore, has outlawed concubinage, raised the legal age of marriage and introduced financial and other penalties for couples who have too many children. In India in the 1970s the late Sanjay Ghandi's sterilization campaigns provoked a backlash which helped to topple an already unpopular government. It seems that China too has had some hostile reactions to state-supported birth-control campaigns. Thus, according to *The Times*:

> the 'one is fine' . . . campaign that advocates single-child families . . . has run into deeply rooted resistance. . . . Parents who promise to have only one child earn for themselves the private plots, and food and fuel supplies of a two-child family. . . . in order to have a second child a woman must run the gauntlet of intimidating interviews with her unit leader and risk the opprobrium of her peers for the chance to take her turn in the unit's pregnancy rota. For the birth of a second child is becoming an act of political defiance.[13]

The article continues with a story, said to have been taken from a Chinese press report, concerning

> the determination of one peasant woman to continue a second pregnancy despite the equally strong pressure from a unit leader to abort. . . . she was eventually forced to have her illegal child in the fields. . . . the leader followed her and strangled the new-born. In revenge the mother went to his home and strangled all three of his children with a piece of wire.[14]

The story is strange and terrible and yet strangely familiar. For is it not a sort of distorted echo of all those earlier stories and legends about the births and deaths of illegitimate children?

Notes and References

CHAPTER 1 DEFINITION, MEANING, EXPLANATION

1 T. D. Eliot and A. R. Hillman (eds.), *Norway's Families*, Philadelphia, 1960.
2 This was Mr James White's Bill: *The Children Act 1979*, London, HMSO, 1978.
3 Koran, surah 81: 8–9.
4 St Augustine, 'The Good of Marriage', *Treatises on Marriage and Other Subjects* (trans. C. T. Wilcox and others, ed. R. J. Deferrari), New York, 1955, pp. 9f.
5 Published first in London in 1932.
6 Published first in London in 1949.
7 Kingsley Davies, 'Illegitimacy and the Social Structure', *American Journal of Sociology*, vol. XLV (1939–40), pp. 215ff.

CHAPTER 2 CAUSES

1 Percy G. Kammerer, *The Unmarried Mother*, London, 1918.
2 ibid., p. 2.
3 ibid., pp. 22, 26.
4 ibid., cases 17 (p. 125), 23 (p. 140), 26 (p. 148), 56 (p. 226).
5 ibid., case 25 (p. 144).
6 ibid., p. 68.
7 ibid., pp. 27–8.
8 ibid., pp. 142f.
9 ibid.
10 ibid., pp. 134f.
11 ibid., p. 221.
12 Kingsley Davis, 'Illegitimacy and the Social Structure', *American Journal of Sociology*, vol. XLV (1939–40), pp. 215ff.; Kingsley Davis, *Human Society*, New York, 1966.

13 Clark E. Vincent, *Unmarried Mothers*, New York and London, 1963.
14 ibid., p. 8.
15 ibid., p. 11.
16 Barbara Thompson, 'Social Study of Illegitimate Maternities', *British Journal of Preventive Social Medicine*, vol. 10 (1956), pp. 75ff.
17 Derek Gill, *Illegitimacy, Sexuality and the Status of Women*, Oxford, 1977, p. 330.
18 Margaret Wynn, *Fatherless Families*, London, 1964.
19 Dennis Marsden, *Mothers Alone*, London, 1969.

CHAPTER 3 ILLEGITIMACY AND THE LAW

1 See, for example, Edmund Leach, *Rethinking Anthropology*, London School of Economics monograph, London, 1961.
2 F. M. Bromley, *Family Law*, London, 1971, p. 26.
3 Age of Marriage Act, Statutes 1929, p. 776.
4 Marriage Act, Statutes 1836, p. 917.
5 Marriage Act, Statues 1823, p. 3.
6 Leviticus 18: 16.
7 Deuteronomy 25: 5.
8 Matrimonial Causes Act, Statutes 1857, p. 637.
9 Matrimonial Causes Act, Statutes 1937, p. 729.
10 Marriage Act, Statutes 1949, vol. II, p. 1621.
11 Matrimonial Causes Act, Statutes 1965, vol. II, p. 1581.
12 Family Law Reform Bill, Statutes 1969, vol. I, p. 997.
13 *Poulett Peerage Case*, Law Reports, Appeal Court, House of Lords, 1903, p. 395.
14 Legitimacy Declaration Act, Statutes 1858, p. 455.
15 *The Times* Law Reports, 12 April 1976.
16 See note 11.
17 *McClellan v. McClellan*, SLT (Scottish Law Times), 1958, p. 12.
18 Deuteronomy 22: 25, 26.
19 See notes 10 and 11.
20 First Succession Act, 25 Henr. VIII, c. 22; see J. R. Tanner, *Tudor Constitutional Documents*, Cambridge, 1948, p. 382.
21 Second Succession Act, 28 Henr. VIII, c. 7; see Tanner, *Tudor Constitutional Documents*, p. 389.
22 Third Succession Act, 35 Henr. VIII, c. 1; see Tanner, *Tudor Constitutional Documents*, p. 397.
23 Act of Recognition. . ., 1 Eliz. I, c. 3; see G. W. Prothero, *Statutes and Constitutional Documents 1558–1625*, Oxford, 1913, p. 21.

24 Bromley, *Family Law*, p. 238 and footnote.
25 Legitimacy Act, Statutes 1926, p. 517.
26 Legitimacy Act, Statutes 1959, p. 1424.
27 Adoption of Infants Act, Statutes 1926, p. 245.
28 See Statutes on inheritance and guardianship prior to 1926.
29 Adoption Act, Statutes 1958, p. 1113.
30 Bromley, *Family Law*, p. 249n.
31 ibid., p. 252n.
32 *Re W, an Infant*, Law Reports, House of Lords, 1971, vol. II, p. 49.
33 *The German Civil Code* (trs. J. S. Forrester, S. M. Goren and H. M. Ilgen), vol. 4, Amsterdam, 1975, paras. 1723–7.
34 Koran, surah 33.
35 Sir Edward Coke, *Third Institute* (1669 edn), p. 211.

CHAPTER 4 THE CUSTODY OF LEGITIMATE CHILDREN

1 Max Käser, *Roman Private Law* (trs. R. Dannenberg), London, 1965, *passim*.
2 Sir William Holdsworth, *History of English Law*, vol. 2, London, 1903–1937, *passim*.
3 Holdsworth, *History of English Law*, vols. 2 and 3, *passim*.
4 Holdsworth, *History of English Law*, vol. 4.
5 Matrimonial Causes Act, Statutes 1857, p. 637.
6 Law Reform (Married Women and Tortfeasors) Act, Statutes 1935, p. 314.
7 Custody of Children Act, Statutes 1839, p. 518.
8 See note 5.
9 F. M. Bromley, *Family Law*, London, 1971, p. 204n.
10 Married Women's Property Act, Statutes 1870, p. 577.
11 Married Women's Property Act, Statutes 1893, p. 334.
12 Married Women's Property Act, Statutes 1908, p. 65.
13 Custody of Infants Act, Statutes 1873, p. 142.
14 Judicature Act, Statutes 1875, p. 759.
15 Custody of Infants Act, Statutes 1886, p. 55.
16 Matrimonial Causes Act, Statutes 1923, p. 280.
17 Guardianship of Infants Act, Statutes 1925, vol. II, p. 1162.
18 See note 6.
19 Matrimonial Causes Act, Statutes 1937, p. 729.
20 Guardianship of Minors Act, Statutes 1971, vol. I, p. 6.
21 R. B. Sheridan, *The Rivals*, Act I, scene ii.
22 Alice Acland, *Caroline Norton*, London, 1948, p. 89.
23 ibid., pp. 118ff.
24 Sung by Robert Tear.

25 Married Women's Property Act, Statutes 1882, p. 454.
26 Representation of the People Act, Statutes 1867, vol. II, p. 936.
27 J. S. Mill, *The Subjection of Women*, London, 1929, p. 248.
28 *Herald*, 26 June 1980.

CHAPTER 5 THE FILIUS NULLIUS RULE

1 Leviticus 20: 10; Deuteronomy 22: 22.
2 Deuteronomy 22: 28, 29.
3 Samuel 11.
4 Plutarch, *Lives of the Noble Grecians and Romans*, vol. 1, Loeb Classical Library, London, 1914, pp. 339, 345.
5 Max Käser, *Roman Private Law* (trs. R. Dannenberg), London, 1965, *passim*.
6 *The Earliest Norwegian Laws* (trs. L. Larsen), New York, 1935, *passim*.
7 *The German Civil Code* (trs. J. S. Forrester, S. M. Goren and H. M. Ilgen), vol. 4, Amsterdam, 1975, paras. 1723–7.
8 Einhard, *Life of Charlemagne* (trs. Samuel Epes Turner), Ann Arbor, Michigan, 1972, pp. 45ff., 71–2.
9 Anthony Wagner, *English Genealogy*, Oxford, 1972, pp. 239ff
10 Davis Douglas (ed.), *English Historical Documents*, vol. 4, London, 1969, p. 343.
11 *Concise Dictionary of National Biography* (ed. Sir Sidney Lee), Oxford, 1903, p. 227.
12 Samuel Pepys, *Diary* (ed. H. B. Wheatley), vol. 7, London, 1896, p. 39.
13 Douglas, *English Historical Documents*, vol. 11 (1971), p. 790.
14 First published in book form in 1852.
15 Cited in G. C. Coulton, *The Medieval Village*, Cambridge, 1925, p. 330.
16 ibid.
17 ibid., p. 469.
18 *Merchet* is Old Norman French for 'market'; see *Oxford English Dictionary*.
19 *Leyrwite* or *lairwite* means 'fine for lying with'; see *Oxford English Dictionary*.
20 F. D. Logan, *Excommunication and the Secular Arm in Medieval England*, Toronto, 1967, *passim*.
21 E. R. C. Brinkworth, *Shakespeare and the Bawdy Court at Stratford*, London, 1972, *passim*.
22 *Paston Letters* (ed. James Gairdner), vol. 6, London, 1904, p. 52.
23 Sidney Webb and Beatrice Webb, *The Old Poor Law*, London, 1927, p. 41.

24 Cited in ibid., p. 49.
25 ibid., p. 201.
26 The novel was first published in 1837–8.
27 Cited in Webb and Webb, *The Old Poor Law*, p. 241.
28 The novel was first published in 1749.
29 Webb and Webb, *The Old Poor Law*, p. 311.
30 *Report from HM Commissioners for Inquiring into the Administration and Practical Operation of the Poor Laws*, 1834.
31 The history of these amendments is described in detail by Ursula Henriques in 'Bastardy and the New Poor Law', *Past and Present*, vol. 37 (1967), pp. 103–29.
32 Registration of Births Act, Statutes 1836, p. 933.
33 *R. v. Nash, re Carey*, Law Reports 10, Queen's Bench Division, 1883, p. 454.
34 *Barnardo v. McHugh*, 1891; see *R. v. Barnardo, Jones' Case*, Law Reports, Appeal Court, House of Lords, 1891, p. 388.
35 See note 34.
36 *Humphries v. Polak and Wife*, Law Reports, vol. II, King's Bench Division, 1901, p. 385.
37 *Re D, an Infant*, All England Law Reports, Court of Appeal, vol. II, 1959, p. 716.
38 Adoption of Children Act, Statutes 1926, p. 245.
39 Adoption of Children Act, Statutes 1949, vol. II, p. 2175; Adoption of Children Act, Statutes 1950, p. 404.
40 Adoption Act, Statutes 1958, p. 1113.
41 F. M. Bromley, *Family Law*, London, 1971, p. 247.
42 Lord Hailsham (ed.), *Halsbury's Statutes of England*, vol. 1, 4th edn, London, 1971, p. 390, paras. 667ff.

CHAPTER 6 MARRIAGE

1 E. E. Evans-Pritchard, *Kinship and Marriage among the Nuer*, Oxford, 1951, ch. 3, sect. 6.
2 ibid.
3 The Areoi were a religious society or brotherhood described by early explorers in the South Seas. Their rituals were said to include sexual orgies and gruesome initiation ceremonies. Women who joined had to promise to kill at birth any infants that they might bear while members of the Areoi society.
4 See, for example, Asen Balikci, *The Netsilik Eskimo*, New York, 1970, *passim*.
5 ibid., *passim*.
6 Kathleen Gough, 'Is the Family Universal?', in N. Bell and E. F. Vogel (eds.), *A Modern Introduction to the Family*, New York, 1968, pt 1, ch. 5.

CHAPTER 7 FAMILY

1 Kingsley Davis, 'Illegitimacy and the Social Structure', *American Journal of Sociology*, vol. XLV (1939–40), pp. 215ff.
2 Kingsley Davis, *Human Society*, New York, 1966, pp. 79ff.
3 B. Malinowski, 'Kinship', *Encyclopedia Britannica*, vol. 13, 14th edn, London and New York, 1929, pp. 403ff.
4 ibid.
5 Rudyard Kipling, *The Light that Failed*, London, 1908, p. 131.
6 See, for example, Nathaniel Hawthorne, *The Scarlet Letter* (1850), ch. 6; Fyodor Dostoyevsky, *The Brothers Karamazov* (1880), bk 3, ch. 6.
7 Koran, surah 16: 57–8.
8 Cf. Jack Goody, 'Kinship', *International Encyclopedia of the Social Sciences*, New York, 1968, pp. 401–7.
9 D. F. Aberle 'Navaho' in D. M. Schneider and E. K. Gough (eds) *Matrilineal Kinship*, Berkeley, Calif., 1962, pp. 96f.
10 Cf. Goody, 'Kinship'.
11 B. Malinowski, *Sex and Repression in Savage Society*, New York, 1927, *passim*.
12 A. I. Richards, 'Some Types of Family Structure Amongst the Central Bantu', in A. R. Radcliffe-Brown and C. Forde (eds.), *African Systems of Kinship and Marriage*, Oxford, 1958, pp. 207ff.
13 Quoted by Virginia Cowles in *The Rothschilds*, London, 1973, p. 43.
14 According to Edith Clarke in *The Mother who Fathered Me*, London, 1957.
15 *Fireflies*, London, 1970, is set in Trinidad.
16 Clarke, *My Mother who Fathered Me*, pp. 113ff., appendices 2, 3, 5 and 7.
17 ibid., *passim*.
18 M. Herskovits, *Life of a Haitian Village*, New York, 1937; *Trinidad Village*, New York, 1947; *Collected Papers*, New York, 1966.
19 Clarke, *My Mother who Fathered Me*.
20 See Lucy Mair, *New Societies*, London, 1963, ch. 3.
21 The Nayar are monogamous nowadays; see C. J. Fuller, *The Nayar Today*, Cambridge, 1977.
22 D. M. Schneider and E. K. Gough (eds.), *Matrilineal Kinship*, Berkeley, Calif., 1962, pt 1, chs. 6, 7; pt 2, *passim*.; E. K. Gough, 'Is the Family Universal?', in Bell and Vogel, *A Modern Introduction to the Family*, pt 1, ch. 5.
23 Gough, 'Is the Family Universal?', p. 86.

CHAPTER 8 THE DISABILITIES OF ILLEGITIMACY

1 See An Act to Enable Bastards in Scotland to Make Testaments, Statutes 1836, p. 25.
2 Quoted in David Douglas (ed.), *English Historical Documents*, vol. 11, London, 1971, p. 635.
3 For instance, one hospital was named the City of London Lying-In Hospital for Married Women; another, the British Lying-In Hospital, stated that its beds were reserved for married women.
4 Personal communication from a doctor.
5 H. D. Eliot and T. D. Hillman (eds.), *Norway's Families*, Philadelphia, 1960, p. 255.
6 *Please Ms*! (National Council for One-Parent Families publication), London 1974.
7 Charles Chaplin, *My Autobiography*, Oxford, 1964.
8 A. M. McWhinnie, *Adopted Children: How They Grow Up*, London, 1967, pp. 4–5.
9 Leo Tolstoy, *Resurrection* (trs. Louise and Aylmer Maude), London, 1903, *passim*.
10 Statutes 1872, p. 245.
11 Statutes 1897, p. 174.
12 Statutes 1874, p. 437.
13 Children Act, Statutes 1908, p. 453.
14 *The Times*, 4 January 1909.
15 *Report of HM Commission on the Poor Laws, 1909–10*, British Parliamentary Paper No. 1910/51/i, p. 144.
16 ibid.
17 McWhinnie, *Adopted Children: How They Grow Up*, pp. 4, 271.
18 ibid., p. 5.
19 *A Directory of Accommodation*, NCOPF publication, London, 1974.
20 Statutes 1862, p. 275.
21 Statutes 1870, p. 443.
22 See, for example, *Barnardo v. McHugh*, 1891; *R. v. Barnardo, Jones' Case*, Law Reports 1981, House of Lords, p. 388.
23 Janet Hitchman, *The King of the Barbareens*, London, 1960, ch. 7.
24 Frank Norman, *Banana Boy*, London, 1969, pp. 101, 105, 133.
25 Harry Bakwin, 'Emotional Deprivation in Infants', *Journal of Pediatrics* (1949), *passim*.
26 John Bowlby, *Maternal Care and Child Health*, Geneva, 1952, *passim*.
27 McWhinnie, *Adopted Children: How They Grow Up*; C. J.

Adcock, *Fundamentals of Psychology*, London, 1960.
28 Bowlby, *Maternal Care and Child Health*, p. 100.
29 Angela Hamblin (ed.), *The Other Side of Adoption*, London, 1977.
30 ibid.
31 Kenneth Soddy, contribution to *Human Rights of Those Born out of Wedlock*, London, 1968.
32 M. Bramall, 'The NCOPF', in Dulan Barrer (ed.), *One-Parent Families*, London, 1975, pp. 161ff.
33 Barrer, *One-Parent Families*, pp. 113ff.
34 *Sunday Telegraph* Colour Supplement, 18 January 1981.

CHAPTER 9 ILLEGITIMACY IN LITERATURE

1 Oscar Wilde, *The Importance of Being Earnest*, Act I.
2 ibid.
3 ibid.
4 ibid.
5 Peter Cook and Dudley Moore, 'Pete and Dud on Sex', in *Once Moore with Cook*, Decca Recording Company, London, 1966.
6 Charles Dickens, *Martin Chuzzlewit*, Oxford, 1975, p. 341
7 *King Lear, passim.*
8 Plato, *Gorgias*, 470–1.
9 Judges 8: 30–1.
10 Judges 9: 4–5.
11 *The Tempest*, Act V, scene i, 11. 269–72.
12 *The Scarlet Letter*, ch. 6.
13 *Henry VI, Part I*, Act V, scene iv, 1. 70.
14 *The Winter's Tale*, Act II, scene iii, 11. 92–5.
15 Hesketh Pearson, *The Life of Oscar Wilde*, London, 1946, p. 236.
16 G. B. Shaw, *Prefaces*, London, 1934, p. 220.
17 ibid., p. 219.
18 ibid., p. 224.

CHAPTER 10 RELIGION

1 Genesis 1: 28.
2 *Encyclopedia of the Jewish Religion* (ed. R. J. Werblowsky and G. Wigoder), Jerusalem, 1966, p. 250.
3 ibid., p. 86.
4 Menachem Elon, *The Principles of Jewish Law*, Jerusalem, 1975, p. 350.
5 Deuteronomy 23: 17.

6 Elon, *The Principles of Jewish Law*, p. 379.
7 *Laws of the State of Israel*, Women's Equal Rights Law, 1951; Succession Law, 1956.
8 H. E. Baker, *The Legal System of Israel*, Jerusalem, 1968, pp. 159–82.
9 *Laws of the State of Israel*, Adoption Law, 1960.
10 Deuteronomy 24: 1.
11 Elon, *The Principles of Jewish Law*, pp. 414ff.
12 *Laws of the State of Israel*, Succession Law, 1956; Elon, *The Principles of Jewish Law*, p. 376.
13 Deuteronomy 23: 2.
14 Elon, *The Principles of Jewish Law*, pp. 430, 435.
15 J. A. Abbo and J. D. Hannan, *The Sacred Canons*, vol. 1, St. Louis, 1952, introduction.
16 See Austin Flannery (ed.), *Vatican Council II*, Dublin, 1977, p. 508.
17 Matthew 19: 12; 1 Corinthians 7: 6, 7, 8.
18 Pius XI, 'Christian Marriage' (Encyclical Letter, 1930).
19 Mgr Pietro Palazzini, 'Marriage', in *Dictionary of Moral Theology*, Rome and London, 1957, pp. 731f.
20 Canons 1012–143; J. Noonan, *Power to Dissolve*, Cambridge, Mass., 1972, *passim*.
21 Corinthians 7: 12–17.
22 G. A. Maloney SJ, 'Oeconomia: a Corrective to Law', *Catholic Lawyer*, vol. 17, no. 2 (1971), pp. 90–109.
23 Paul VI, 'Mixed Marriage' (Apostolic Letter, 1970); see also Flannery, *Vatican Council II*, pp. 481 and 508.
24 Canons 1116 and 1138.
25 N. J. Coulson, *A History of Islamic Law*, Edinburgh 1964, chs 1 and 2, *passim*.
26 See e.g. N. J. Coulson, *Succession in the Muslim Family*, Cambridge, 1971, *passim*.
27 Koran, surah 2: 223f; surah 65
28 Koran, surah 4: 24; surah 33: 50.
29 Koran, surah 4: 15.
30 Article on 'Zina', *Encyclopedia of Islam*, vol. 4, London, 1929.
31 Jeremiah 9: 2.
32 Ezekiel, 23: 3, 12, 14, 16, 17.
33 Isaiah 57: 3, 4, 5.
34 Revelation 17: 5.

CHAPTER 11 THE ABOLITION OF ILLEGITIMACY

1 See Crane Brinton, *French Revolutionary Laws on Illegitimacy*,

Cambridge, Mass., 1936.
2 ibid., p. 53.
3 ibid., p. 52.
4 ibid., p. 61.
5 Vladimir Gsovski, *Soviet Civil Law*, Ann Arbor, Michigan, 1948–9, contains English translations of the Soviet Codes referred to in this section.
6 Gsovski, *Soviet Civil Law*, vol. 1, p. 127.
7 For example, *The Housewife and the Town Hall*, London, 1934; *The Economic Position of the Married Woman*, Oxford, 1924.
8 *Report of the Registrar–General for England and Wales*, 1916.
9 Statistics taken from Lettice Fisher, *21 Years and After*, London. 1939.
10 ibid., pp. 7–8.
11 *Report of the Committee on One-Parent Families*, London, 1974. The committee was chaired by Sir Morris Finer.
12 Dulan Barrer (ed.), *One-Parent Families*, London, 1975, p. 15.
13 T. D. Eliot and A. R. Hillman, *Norway's Families*, Philadelphia, 1960, *passim*.
14 Percy G. Kammerer, *The Unmarried Mother*, London, 1918. p. xii.
15 Anders Agell, in *Scandinavian Studies in Law 1980*, vol. 24, Stockholm, 1980, p. 11.
16 ibid., p. 47.

CHAPTER 12 ILLEGITIMACY AND ILLICIT BIRTH

1 L. Wittgenstein, *Philosophical Investigations* (trs. G. E. M. Anscombe), Oxford, 1953, paras. 66–7.
2 ibid.
3 J. R. Bambrough, 'Universals and Family Resemblance', in George Pitcher (ed.), *Wittgenstein*, London, 1970, pp. 186–204.
4 In lectures in Cambridge, 1977–8.
5 See chapter 6.
6 See chapter 2.
7 Jack Goody, *Comparative Studies in Kinship*, London, 1969, ch. 2, *passim*.
8 ibid., p. 23
9 ibid., p. 15.
10 ibid., p. 16.
11 See chapters 7, 8.
12 See chapter 10.

13 *The Times*, 13 February 1981. The article, written by Dinah Lee, appeared in a supplement on China.
14 ibid.

Index